365 One-Minute Golf Lessons

365 One-Minute Golf Lessons

Quick and Easy Stroke-Saving Tips and Exercises

Robin McMillan

A John Boswell Associates Book
HarperCollins*Publishers*

HarperCollins books may be purchased for educational, business, or sales promotional use. For information please write: Special Markets Department, HarperCollins Publishers, Inc., 10 East 53rd Street, New York, NY 10022.

FIRST EDITION

Designed by Barbara Cohen Aronica

Library of Congress Cataloging-in-Publication Data

McMillan, Robin.
365 one-minute golf lessons : quick and easy stroke-saving tips / Robin McMillan. — 1st ed.
p. cm.
Includes index.
ISBN 0-06-017087-5
1. Golf. I. Title. II. Title: Three hundred sixty-five one-minute golf lessons.
GV965.M346 1994
796.352—dc20 94-4834

---

94 95 96 97 98 10 9 8 7 6 5 4 3 2 1

Contents

Introduction

In the summer of 1988, I had the pleasure of watching Severiano Ballesteros blister Nick Price in the final round of the British Open. Ballesteros was gracious in victory, proclaiming to the world's golf media that his Zimbabwean opponent may have been the loser on that day but nevertheless was on the verge of winning a major championship of his own.

We knew this. It was common knowledge that Price was already working with a well-known tutor to reconstruct a golf swing that, despite his moderate success around the world, had an annoying habit of breaking down in the heat of battle. Price felt he needed a swing that was so grooved and robotic that, no matter how nervous he became, the swing would perform exactly as programmed.

Two years later, over breakfast at a country club just north of New York City, I suggested to Price—who had not won a single tournament in the interim—that perhaps this new swing thing was taking too long to show up. Perhaps he was barking up the wrong flagstick.

No, he earnestly replied, it was just a matter of time. He would stick with the program no matter how long it took because, as success in major championships is the true measure of a great golfer, this was a clear case of better late than never.

Fast forward *another* two years. Nick Price wins his major at last, the 1992 PGA Championship. Then he starts to win everything he enters. During one torrid, four-week stretch, he signs up for three tournaments and wins the lot of them—and no one had done *that* since 1980 (Tom Watson, in case you're interested).

So all this got me thinking that maybe I had it all wrong. Maybe I should turn pro, hire a swing guru, play at least six rounds of golf, put in a further 15–20 hours a week on the practice range, hitting a hundred or so practice balls per day.

I'd do what Price did. I'd totally rebuild my swing. I'd program it. Polish it. Perfect it. Roboticize it. And it would take me only, oh, five years?

Five years?

I should be so fortunate (not to mention rich). Perhaps the top pros can afford such a strategy, but the rest of us are just straight out of luck and, more important, out of time. We consider ourselves blessed if we can squeeze in 15 minutes on a driving range before a weekend fourball. Thirty minutes? Were we to drop dead on the spot, at least we would die happy.

And even when we do find a minute or two to practice, all we tend to do is turn small swing problems into complete catastrophes. To 99 percent of the golfing world, the concept of taking time to develop a good golf swing is just not up for discussion.

We do have an option, however, and that is to learn the golf swing and golf strategy piece by piece. What was it they used to say about the playing style of baseball's St. Louis Cardinals? "A nick here, a nick there, and pretty soon you're bleeding to death." This book is similar, only the maxim becomes "A quick lesson here, a quick lesson there, and pretty soon you'll have yourself a golf game."

The lessons, however, must have a firm grounding in golfing logic and the laws of physics, which for all we know may be one and the same. Each lesson must be simple, sensible, and easily applied. And each must have legs, for what good is a lesson that works for a few rounds, but leads to other problems thereafter.

365 One-Minute Golf Lessons is based on this simple wisdom. It is arranged to cover every aspect of the game, and never will you need more than 60 seconds to grasp a particular shot or a particular piece of advice. You'll become a better thinker both on and off the golf course, and your mechanics will improve immensely. And time will no longer be an issue.

And that's all you need, really, to put a hefty dent in all those annoying golf scores.

ONE

Basic Lessons

1 Basic Grips

Almost every golfer uses one of two basic grips, the Vardon, or overlap, grip and the interlocking grip. A few players prefer a third grip, the baseball grip. Choose the one with which you are most *comfortable.*

• **The Vardon (or Overlap) Grip.** With the left hand on the grip of the club—you should be able to see two and a half knuckles—place the right hand on the club so that the left thumb fits snugly below the base of the right thumb. Place the left pinkie over the division between the right index and middle fingers. This is the "overlap." Most good players use this grip.

• **The Interlocking Grip.** Follow the instructions for the Vardon grip, but instead of overlapping the pinkie, wrap it under and around the index finger.

It is generally thought that this grip allows too much wrist action, giving the golfer a tendency to hook the ball. But the Vardon grip can be a tough proposition for golfers with small hands, as evidenced by the fact that Jack Nicklaus interlocks.

- **The "Baseball" Grip.** The fingers neither overlap nor interlock—every finger touches the grip of the club.

2 The Basic Address

- **Width of Stance.** The widest—just beyond shoulder width—your feet should be is when you hit driver. The shorter the club you're hitting, the narrower your stance becomes.

- **Distance from the Ball.** With a club in your hand, stand up straight. Now bend the knees slightly and put the club on the ground. *That* is how far you should stand from the ball. In other words, the length of the club determines the distance. Thus, the shorter the club, the closer you'll stand.

- **Ball Position.** Some golfers insist that you play the ball in the same position for every shot. But the general rule is that you should play the ball opposite your left heel for woods and long irons and toward the middle of your stance for middle irons. Open your stance and play the ball almost off your back heel for short-iron shots.

• **Head Position.** For full shots, your head should remain slightly behind the ball. In some instances, usually on greenside chips, you'll play the ball back in you stance and your head will naturally be ahead of the ball.

• **Shoulder Position.** Your right shoulder should be slightly below your left.

3 Basic Alignment

There are three alignments:

1. In a *square* stance, an imaginary line drawn from your right toe to your left toe is parallel to the target line.

2. In an *open* stance, the left foot is drawn back from this imaginary line.

3. In a *closed* stance, the right foot is drawn back from the line.

4 The Basic Swing

Begin the backswing by drawing back the clubhead low to the ground. Do not break the wrists and do not "pick up" the club with your hands. As the backswing progresses, the wrists should break naturally.

Pause slightly when the club reaches the top of the swing and the shaft of the club is approximately parallel to the ground. At this point your weight should be concentrated on the inside of your right leg.

Your hips should lead the downswing, followed by your shoulder and arms. As the club swings through the impact area, your arms should straighten, your hips should open up, and your weight should shift to your left side. As you finish your swing, the only part of your right foot that should be touching the ground is your toe.

5 The Basic Drive

Tee the ball so that its center is just above the top of your clubhead. The ball should be opposite your left heel so you make contact on the upswing. Swing the club back slowly and low to the ground.

6 The Basic Fairway Wood, Long-Iron, and Middle-Iron Shots

Play the ball a few inches inside your left heel. Much is made of hitting the ball with a sweeping motion, but that leads to tops (hitting the top of the ball). It's better to think of hitting down and through. Above all, however, remain steady throughout the swing.

7 The Basic Short-Iron Shot

Short-iron shots differ considerably, based primarily on the lie, the distance to the hole, the hazards, and the weather conditions. But certain fundamentals apply to all short-iron shots:

1. Open your stance slightly.

2. Flex your knees more than usual (the shorter club length almost forces you to do this).

3. On a full short-iron shot, finish the backswing in the three-quarter position, with the club pointing up and over your head.

4. Avoid hand or wrist action except on the most delicate shots.

5. Hit with a descending blow.

TWO

The Grip

Proper Pressure

How tightly should you grip a golf club? Not, as J.C. Snead once put it, "so tight you could hear the cows screaming." Perhaps, as Seve Ballesteros suggests, "as tightly as you need to squeeze a tube of toothpaste to make the toothpaste come out." Or, as Sam Snead says, no tighter than you would hold a small bird.

As you can see, you shouldn't hold a golf club tightly at all. If you do, it is almost inevitable that you will lose your grip on the club at the top of your swing. Tight hands also mean tight forearms, which in turn mean a tight upper body. So it's almost impossible to make a fluid, relaxed swing.

You should be especially aware of grip pressure in tense situations. During a tournament, or when about to hit a high-risk shot, you may unwittingly grip too tightly—a fault familiar even to the pros. On the final morning of the 1986 British Open Greg Norman's friend—and sort of mentor—Jack

Nicklaus, gave him one piece of advice: Concentrate on light grip pressure.

Norman cruised to victory.

9 Palm Reading

After you've played a few rounds of golf with the same glove, examine it to see how the palm and fingers are worn down. This information can tell you what's right or wrong with your grip.

The golfer whose glove is wearing thin on the last three fingers and the area of the palm directly below them is gripping the club correctly: He's applying light pressure with the last three fingers of the left hand. These are the fingers that control the club during the swing. When they're working properly, the hands, arms, and shoulders are free to work together to allow a smooth, steady, and powerful motion.

Golfers whose gloves are wearing down on the pad and the base of the thumb are gripping the club in their palms. This is wrong. It's almost impossible to keep a good grip on the club at the top of the swing. To compensate, the golfer squeezes with the thumb and cuts short the backswing. He is out of rhythm, gets jerky, and is not likely to hit the ball well.

10 The No-Wrinkle Grip

A good way to tell if your hands are at the correct height at address is to examine your wrists for wrinkles: There should be no "wrinkles" at the backs of your wrists when you grip the club.

If you're holding the grip of the club too low to the ground, your wrists will be cocked slightly and you'll see wrinkles circling your wrists at the base of your thumbs.

If your hands are too far from the ground, you won't see wrinkles on your wrists, but check the pad of your left palm; you will find wrinkles where the hand joins the wrist.

11 Pray for a Good Grip

Although it may sound blasphemous, the best way to position the hands properly on the grip is to pray.

As you hold the club, position your hands with the palms facing each other. Now just move them together until they're gripping the club.

You are now in position to adopt the interlocking or the overlap grip. Slide your right hand below the left and do all the necessary fingerwork. Just make sure that the palms remain parallel.

12 Look, Ma—No Thumb!

The position of the right thumb on the grip of the golf club is crucial to holding the club properly.

Golfers who position the right thumb on the right side of the grip (looking down at the thumb after you've taken your grip) have a grip that is too strong and that will inevitably produce a hook.

And those players who position the right thumb squarely on top of the grip may have their hands in a better position, but they're allowing the thumb to be dominant and that, too, could produce a hook.

When correctly placed, the right thumb wraps over the club toward the point where the right index finger curls up the underside. It can even touch the index finger. This position effectively takes the right thumb out of play and allows the last three fingers of the right hand to work properly—as a good grip should do.

THREE

Address

The Right Kind of Waggle

Waggling—that is, moving the club back and forth slightly without actually striking the ball—before you start your backswing prepares the muscles for the upcoming swing. It's a good move to make, but not many golfers tailor their waggle to the *type* of shot they're about to hit.

If you intend to hit your ball straight, and take the club straight back along the target line to start the backswing, you should waggle along that line. If you intend to cut or slice the ball, and intend to start the backswing outside the target line, you should waggle outside the line. And if you intend to draw or hook the ball and want to start the club back inside the target line, you should waggle inside it.

This way you'll prepare your muscles for the proper backswing before you actually make your stroke.

14 Poetry in Motion

Tension is the enemy of every golfer, amateur or pro, and it is most dangerous when you are standing over a tee shot. At such times you need maximum distance, so you must be relaxed enough to release all your body's energy.

The best way to stay loose, therefore, is to do just that: Stay loose. *Keep moving.*

We're not advising that you start break-dancing. Just move something slightly. Most players like to waggle the club at address, which not only helps them stay loose but also gives them a sense of releasing the wrists and passing the clubhead through the impact area. Others like to bob their knees. Still others wiggle their toes or shake their rear ends slightly.

But it doesn't really matter what you move. The point is that you don't give yourself a chance to stiffen up.

15 The Backhand Slap

To ensure a square clubface at impact, think of the back of your left hand as the clubface, and position it parallel to the actual clubface at address.

Line up the club square to the target line, then take your stance. Now adjust your grip accordingly. When you swing down and through, make sure that the back of your hand returns to its original position. Unless you've regripped during the swing, you should meet the ball squarely.

16 The Right Way

What's your routine when you step up to the ball? Do you position your feet and then place the club behind the ball? Or do you put the clubface behind the ball with your left hand and then lead into your stance with your left foot? If you do the latter, you're like most golfers—and you're putting yourself at a disadvantage from the outset. Golfers who position the club with the left hand have a tendency to lower the left shoulder too far and that causes all kinds of problems, a significant one being that it's tough to make a full turn on the backswing.

It's a far better idea to position the club behind the ball *with your right hand,* then lead into your stance with your right foot. Try it. Notice how your right shoulder starts off lower than your left? Now you can swing back freely and effectively.

17 For Your Eyes Only

When you take your stance and address the ball, you likely will want to take a good look at your target. It's part of the aiming process.

What you should *not* do, however, is lift your head to take a look. As a golfer prepares to hit his shot, he should be concentrating on it, mentally and physically, and raising the head also raises the shoulders and interrupts the process.

It's better just to turn your head to the left and zero in on the target with your left eye. That way your body will stay in the proper position to begin the swing.

18 The Perfect Press

It's not a bad idea to "press" during the address, just before you start your backswing: Make a slight forward movement with your hands to ensure that they are ahead of the ball—their ideal position at impact—before you start your backswing.

But too few golfers realize that pressing correctly is almost as important as swinging correctly. Many players press too far forward, effectively closing the blade of the club and promoting a hook. Others press the club down into the ground and run the risk of catching the club in the grass (or whatever surface they happen to be in) on the backswing.

The perfect press is nothing more than a quarter-inch to half-inch movement with the hands that rocks the swing into action.

19 Pocket Guide

Many teachers and instructional aids emphasize the correct positioning of the V's formed by the index fingers and thumbs as they grip the club. Too few emphasize the importance of where and how the hands should be joined together. When you can make a two-hand grip into a single unit, you'll have a much more solid hold on the club—you'll be able to relax the hands without losing control of the club.

Grip the club with the left hand, with the V pointing at your nose. Now place the base of your right thumb over your left thumb, hold it there, then let the right fingers take their natural place on the grip.

Always keep your left thumb firmly in the pocket in the heel of your right hand and you won't go wrong.

20 Nose Jobs

If you think your nose isn't part of your golf swing, think again. It actually can come in quite handy (and not just to smell blood when your opponent's just hit his eighth shot on the final hole into a ravine).

The position of your nose at address can help you set your weight correctly for low shots, regular shots, and high shots.

For low shots, position your head so that your nose is pointing at the ball. The slight movement will make it easier to shift your weight to your left side—an essential move for hitting low shots.

For regular shots, point your nose at a spot on the ground a few inches behind the ball. Your weight should be evenly distributed.

For high shots, point your nose at a spot even farther back. Now it will be easier to move more of your weight, quite correctly, to your right side.

21 No Grounds for Tension

When you must hit from a difficult lie, don't ground the club when you address the ball.

When you press down on the grass, you tend to get into an "I'll whack this one out of here" frame of mind. You tighten your grip, which in turn tightens your arms, your shoulders, and, worst of all, your entire upper body.

So try to get a mental image of the shot you're about to hit, particularly of the impact area, and then hover the club above the ground slightly. You will want your wrists to be firm at impact, but starting out with too tight a grip is not the way to do it.

22 On Your Knee

A simple way to make sure your club and hands are properly aligned for iron shots is to take your stance and address the ball with your left hand positioned over your left knee.

This alignment of hand and knee not only allows you to stand with an imaginary line running from your left shoulder straight down to a point behind the ball but also helps you keep your hands slightly ahead of the ball at address. Both are necessary components of solid iron play.

23 The Head Press

Ever wondered why Jack Nicklaus and other golfers turn their head slightly to the right before they swing? They're presetting the head so they can make a full shoulder turn and thereby generate more power.

There is a natural tendency to bury the head between the shoulders at address. This action restricts the shoulders from turning fully.

By just turning the head slightly, Nicklaus & Co. still keep their eyes on the ball, but their shoulders don't fight the neck muscles when they turn.

24 The Correct Bend

When you flex your knees at address, keep your shins almost perpendicular to the ground. Your weight will be evenly distributed between the balls of your feet and your heels, and your knees will be sufficiently flexed to allow a strong fluid swing.

If you lean forward as you bend your knees, you put too much weight on the toes. You're likely then to swing from outside to in and cut across the ball, which will result in either a slice (if the clubface is open) or a pull (if the clubface is closed).

If you keep your shins as close as possible to perpendicular to the ground, your weight will be evenly distributed between the balls of your feet and your heels, and your knees will be flexed enough to allow you a strong, fluid swing.

25 Start Correctly

The address is, in the view of many top teachers, the key to hitting the ball consistently well. You cannot expect to hit the ball well if your body is not in the proper position to do so.

Think back to some of the best shots you ever hit. Apart from the result of those shots, you probably remember two things: that you barely felt the ball when you hit it—feeling the ball usually means your nerves are serving your brain notice of a mis-hit; and that you felt great just standing up to the ball.

The two are related, but the first is far more important. While you can feel good but hit the ball badly, you can't hit the ball well without first feeling good.

FOUR

The Swing

From the Mouth of an Expert

The most important element of a swing is not power or strength. It is rhythm, or "tempo," as it is so often called.

Here we defer to the great Bobby Jones, who wrote this in an old golfing magazine:

> The man who hits at the ball has no sense of rhythm. Similarly, the man who, after a short backswing, attempts to make up for lost space by convulsive effort initiating the downstroke has no sense of rhythm. The only one who has a chance to achieve a rhythmic, well-timed stroke is the man who in spite of all else yet swings the clubhead. And the crucial area is where the swing changes direction at the top. If the backswing can be made to flow back leisurely and to an ample length, whence the start downward can be made without the feeling that there may not be enough time left, there is good

chance of success. But a hurried backswing indicates a hurried start downward, and a short backswing makes some sort of rescue effort imperative. A good golfer will not likely be guilty of either.

27 Further Notes on Ball Position

In the section on basics we present two schools of thought about ball position: (1) The ball should be positioned in the same place in the stance—usually opposite the left heel—for all shots; and (2) the shorter the club, the farther back in the stance the ball should be positioned.

Here's a third school: Make a few practice swings at an imaginary ball. It doesn't matter which club you use. Now look at the turf. You scuffed the turf at the *bottom* of your swing arc, so for shots that aren't teed up, the beginning of the scuff mark is where you should position your ball. If the mark differs from club to club, then ball position will differ too.

On shots hit from a tee, you should tee your ball at the end of the scuff mark, because that marks where your swing arc rises.

28 The Plane Truth

One key to a smooth swing is to keep your clubhead on the same swing plane throughout the swing—a lesson made unnecessarily difficult by the fact that most golfers don't know what the swing plane is and therefore don't know how to keep the clubhead on it.

A handy piece of imagery will make the swing plane crystal clear:

Imagine that you are swinging a weight on the end of a piece of rope. Now imagine swinging it so that the rope remains taut throughout your swing. In order for the rope to do that, the weight must stay on the same swing plane.

Now apply the same principle to your golf swing, only now the rope becomes the shaft of your golf club, and the weight becomes the clubhead. As you try to keep the shaft "taut" you'll begin to feel the clubhead more, and when you can feel the clubhead during the swing, you'll be far better equipped to make solid contact with the ball.

Another useful piece of imagery is to think of your swing plane as a huge wheel, with your body as the hub. Your clubhead follows the circumference of the wheel.

29 How Far Back?

In the perfect full swing the club should be swung back until it is parallel to the ground and pointing at the target behind your back. If it doesn't reach parallel, then the golfer hasn't completed the swing and likely will jerk the club down and into the ball. If it goes past parallel, then the swing is too long to control properly.

This is indeed sound advice, but only for those among us who are physically capable of swinging to the perfect position.

Golfers come in all shapes, sizes, and ages, and many golfers, particularly older players, can't reach parallel. Similarly, golfers who are not of perfect build may not be able to raise their hands high enough on the backswing to set the club properly at the top.

In each case the worst thing to do is to force the action in pursuit of the perfect swing. The end result is bad balance and even worse execution.

You'll fare a lot better if you swing the club back as best you can, and focus on good tempo and solid contact. As the saying goes, no one ever hit a golf ball with his backswing.

30 A Good Break

Many teachers preach that the way to get more distance is to "release" through the ball by rolling the right forearm counterclockwise and "over" the left arm as they hit the ball.

It's quite possible to do this—if you're a low-handicap golfer. When the rest of us try it, we end up hooking everything sharply to the left.

Remember, release should happen not at impact but when the hands reach eye level on the follow-through.

As you swing through the ball the back of your left hand should be facing directly down the target line, with your wrists still firm. As you swing through keep the wrists just as firm, with your hands extending down the target line.

Now, as your hands come up to eye level, let the wrists break naturally. In this way you'll extend fully through the ball, and *that* will give you an extra yard or two.

31 Elbow Room

Even though Jack Nicklaus has won every honor in golf with what is known as a "flying right elbow"—the right elbow points out from the right side of the body at the top of the swing—we do not recommend this position. Usually the golfer forces a flying right elbow back in toward his body during the downswing, and that action can pull the clubhead inside the line. To make contact, the golfer then has to swing from inside to out, and *that* is the major cause of hooks.

Here's an exercise that demonstrates the ideal positioning of the right elbow at the top of the swing. Imagine that you're one of those cocktail waiters who carry their trays up high. You carry your tray with your right arm, with the tray roughly level with your right ear. Notice how your right elbow points straight down.

Your right bicep and tricep may feel a little tight, but don't worry. It's natural to feel tightness when making a swing change. The tightness will eventually go away.

32 Turn, Turn, Turn

The two main factors in achieving maximum distance are hitting the ball with the sweet spot—on the nose, as they say—and maximizing the clubhead speed. The former is obvious; the latter is too often misunderstood.

You'll cause more problems than

you'll solve if you try to increase club-head speed by swinging faster. For one thing, you'll rarely hit the ball on the sweet spot! The correct way to get more clubhead speed is to widen the arc of your swing, and you do that by making a full shoulder turn.

Some golfers are just plain scared to make a full shoulder turn. They think they'll lose control, so they start the downswing from the three-quarters position, which causes them to jerk at the ball.

Instead, they should let the swing *flow* to the top, until the clubhead is pointing at the target—with as little hip turn as possible—then uncoil and hit through the ball.

That sort of turn will give you all the speed that you'll need.

33 Unlock the Right Knee

So much importance is put on anchoring the swing around the inside of the right leg that very often the knee stays rigid during the entire swing. This is especially dangerous during the downswing and follow-through because a locked right knee prevents your weight from shifting from the right to the left and causes you to throw your arms at the ball and hit a weak push to the right.

So by all means keep your weight inside your right leg as you reach the top of the swing. But when you begin your downswing, loosen your right knee and let your legs and hips guide you through the ball.

And About the Other Knee . . .

The left knee can play an important role in the swing too. It should be flexible during the backswing, then become a solid base of support during the downswing.

Point your left knee at the ball when you swing back. It doesn't matter whether you keep your left foot planted (which we advise) or raise it.

As you swing down keep your knee firm, but don't straighten the left leg too quickly. This leads to a lifting of the left side and can make you hit your ball thin or top it completely.

35 Hand-Knee Coordination

Problems with the downswing result from two common faults. The arms begin the downswing before the legs have a chance to get moving, and the legs move before the backswing is completed. Here's a way to make sure that the downswing begins and the legs move *at exactly the same time.*

When you reach the top of your backswing, focus on your left hand and your left knee. As you begin to bring your hands down, your left knee should slide to the left, toward the target.

These two focal points will lead the rest of your body into a proper, coordinated swing.

36 Head Game

A quick cure for hitting the ball fat (behind it) or thin (blading it; striking the ball with the leading edge of the clubface) is to work on sensing where your clubhead is throughout the swing. Keep your eye on the ball and your head steady, but keep your mind on the clubhead.

Simple hand-eye coordination will bring the clubhead into the ball in the proper position.

This is also a very good practice drill.

37 Hips First

Golfers tend to be so eager to get their shoulders turning on the downswing that they throw them open and either slice the ball or pull-hook it.

You will hit the ball much straighter if you wait until the hips *make* the shoulders turn. When the downswing begins, the hips should clear (or move counterclockwise) to allow the body to swing through. The shoulders shouldn't really turn at all.

In the best downswing the hips turn first and then lead the shoulders to turn naturally as the ball is struck.

Note that as your shoulders turn, your head will come up; do not try to keep it tucked down at this point.

38 The Quick Peek

What's the best way to tell if you're overswinging—that is, if your club goes beyond parallel to the ground at the top of the backswing?

By looking at it.

You can easily tell if you're going beyond parallel by taking a few practice swings and then taking a quick peek with the left eye as you reach the top of your swing. If you can see your clubhead, you're overswinging.

Now work on that backswing till you can see nothing at all.

39 How to Heel

A good way to control the swing and to coil the body to store energy during the backswing is to keep the left heel anchored firmly to the ground during the entire swing.

All too often golfers raise the left heel during the backswing and then emphatically bring it down to the ground during the downswing. It's a show of force with negative consequences: The body releases the power it has stored during the backswing and sways to the left or lunges during the downswing.

Keep your left heel on the ground to provide a foundation for the firm left side that is fundamental to every solid golf swing.

40 Behind and Through

You'll often hear it said that good golfers "stay behind the ball" during impact, but this can be confusing when you're also told to move your weight to the left and swing through the ball.

How can you be behind and through at the same time?

In fact, staying behind the ball simply means keeping the *head* behind the ball at impact. Were you to draw an imaginary line up from the ball as you make contact, ideally it would graze the left side of your face.

Think of this line when you're swinging and you'll keep your head in the proper position—behind the ball.

41 No Peeking

Earlier we explained that you can tell if you're overswinging by sneaking a peek with the left eye as you reach the top of your swing. That's true—for practice shots.

When you are hitting shots for real, the last thing you should do is look at your golf club.

A good swing begins with the clubhead moving back slowly along the target line, as low to the ground as possible. It sounds simple enough, but an astounding number of golfers actually look at the clubhead to make sure it stays low!

Peeking at this point takes your eyes off the ball, causes your head to move, and generally provides a poor start to the swing.

Try simply to *sense* that the clubhead is low to the ground. The only thing you should look at during the swing is the ball—as you hit it and as it flies toward its target.

42 Loosen the Left

A famous piece of instruction you would do well to ignore recommends that you keep your left arm straight during the swing.

It's true that you don't want to collapse the arm during the backswing, but neither do you want a rigid left arm. Trying for that will so tighten the muscles that you'll end up with a jerky swing instead of a long, flowing one.

Tight muscles do not a golf swing make, so loosen the muscles in your left arm. As you swing back, your arm will stay quite straight as you extend the swing arc up and above your shoulders. But if your left arm bends a little as you reach the top of the swing, that's fine. Your arm muscles will be in far better shape to begin the downswing.

The one part of the swing in which you must have a straight left arm is at impact.

Shake on It

How to tell if you've executed the proper takeaway?

Shake hands on it.

Here's what we mean: Swing a club back as you normally would. When you reach the point where the shaft of the club is parallel to the ground—about a third of the way into the backswing—stop and, using your left hand, take the club out of your right hand.

If your right hand is in the perfect "handshake" position—as though you were shaking hands with someone to your right—your takeaway is just fine. If your palm is facing down, you probably suffer from a flying right elbow. If it's facing up, your swing may be too flat.

But the point here isn't to analyze the fault. It's to encourage you to get your right hand into the ideal position to say hello to lower scores.

44 A Cure for the Slice

Here are some of the major faults that lead to a slice and how to cure them:

FAULT: Your stance is open. This causes you to swing from outside to in, across the ball.
CURE: Stand square to the ball.

FAULT: Your right arm is set higher than your left at address. As you swing down you'll compensate by tucking in the right elbow. This causes you to come across the ball with the clubface open.
CURE: Keep your right elbow close to your body throughout the swing.

FAULT: You rotate your hands clockwise during the takeaway. This opens the face of the club.
CURE: Do not consciously rotate your hands. Maintain the same wrist angle throughout the swing.

FAULT: When you start your downswing, you lunge forward. To compensate (and bring the clubhead back into the ball), you end up swinging from outside to in.
CURE: Initiate the downswing by sliding your hips to the left.

45 Powerful Footwork

In general, it's not a good idea to move your feet much during the golf swing. The feet usually serve primarily as anchors.

But if you take a look at Jack Nicklaus's swing, you'll notice two moves he makes with his feet that could help you.

- *Right Foot.* When Nicklaus addresses a tee shot, he opens his right foot more—that is, he points the toe farther to the right. This in turns helps open his hips when he swings back, and allows a fuller shoulder turn and, therefore, more power.
- *Left Foot.* Nicklaus's left toe points out slightly to his left when he addresses the ball. As he swings back he lifts his left heel. But when he swings down, he plants his heel slightly left of where it started, so now his foot is perpendicular to the target line. This simple move firms up his left side and prevents him from losing the power he built up with his right-foot maneuver.

46 Why You Shouldn't Overswing

John Daly's backswing, in which the clubhead all but bumps into the outside of his left leg, legitimizes the problem of overswinging.

Here's why it's bad: Apart from the fact that longer swings are tougher to control, swinging too far back will more often than not cause you to lose your grip of the club.

Try it. Do you notice how your left hand strains to keep hold of the club? Your grip should never be put under such pressure—especially when the middle, third, and pinkie fingers on the left hand form the most important part of the grip.

So don't overswing and you won't lose your grip.

47 Hands Ahead

We'll keep this one short and simple.

THERE IS NOT A SHOT IN GOLF IN WHICH YOU SHOULD HAVE THE HANDS AHEAD OF THE BALL AT IMPACT.

End of lesson.

The Good and the Bad

Isn't it odd how golfers who hit their woods well hit their irons badly—and vice versa?

If you fit into one of these families, here's how you can fix your fault and hit both types of golf club well:

- *Bad Irons.* Players with this fault are likely to have a sound swing that sweeps the ball well from a tee, and don't do too badly with fairway woods. On each of these shots golfers tend not to hit down on the ball so much (this is the case more with the tee shot than with the fairway wood). The weight tends to stay on the right side through impact. With irons, however, it is vitally important to shift the weight to the left side and hit down and through the ball. So all these golfers have to do when hitting irons is remember to shift left and hit down.

- *Bad Woods.* Although it is correct to hit down on fairway woods, the shot should still be more of a sweep than one hit with irons. Most players who hit woods poorly tend to start hitting down from the top of their swings. Their weight shifts quickly to the left and they hit down too quickly. The key for these players is to work on a full shoulder turn and pivot, and to stay behind the ball.

49 Chin Music

You can ensure a fuller turn by tucking your left shoulder under your chin on the backswing. This is no revelation, however.

What you seldom hear is the same tip applied to the downswing. So here goes: When you swing down and through, *tuck your right shoulder under your chin.*

Don't be so strict about this that you stiffen up completely. Just keep the thought in mind and you'll find that you'll quickly learn the correct movement on the downswing and follow-through.

When You Want to Let It Rip

Although it's never a good idea to try to kill a golf ball—swing too hard and too fast and your chances of hitting the ball solidly are about nil—there will be occasions when you want to put a little muscle into your ball. Perhaps you want to reach a par five or long par four in two, or perhaps a few extra yards could prove the difference between winning or losing a match.

Is there anything you can do to help

you pull off the shot? About the only thing is to put yourself in a position to swing a little harder. By that we mean you should work on a more solid *base.* Widen your stance slightly. That done, you should be able to make a fuller turn without falling to one side or the other and really attack the ball.

51 The Quick Draw (and Fade)

Wouldn't it be wonderful if we could hit perfect shots with a little draw when we want distance—such shots are hit with topspin, which makes the ball roll more on landing—and perfect shots with a little fade when we want the ball to stop quickly?

It's not that difficult. All we're going to do is adjust the swing plane slightly.

For either a draw or a fade, address the ball with a square stance and align yourself *with your target.*

Now, to hit the draw, pick out an imaginary target just to the right of the real one, and without changing anything about your setup, swing as though you were trying to hit that target. Your swing plane will become more inside-outside, and your ball will start to the right and come back to the actual target.

For a slight fade, do likewise so that

your swing plane becomes more outside-in. Now your ball will start left and come back to its target.

What *Is* the Late Hit?

Even the top professionals take years to perfect this move, but it takes only a minute to learn.

In a nutshell, the late hit is really a late straightening of the wrists. As you swing the club down, you maintain the angle—usually ninety degrees—formed by your arms and the club at the top of your swing (arms vertical, club parallel).

If, on the downswing, you uncock the wrists too early, which is to say, at around waist level, you're likely then to strike the ball with your hands too far back; you'll probably blade it.

The late hit, however, means that you keep the top-of-the-swing angle intact until just before impact. It helps you whip the club through the hitting zone, and increases clubhead speed and, therefore, distance.

53 Read All About It

The lettering and numbering on your ball aren't there purely to identify the manufacturer or some resort, or whatever—at least not to you.

They can be used as a bull's-eye for your swing.

Instead of trying to hit the whole ball, tee it up with the lettering at the very back. Then keep your eyes on the lettering as you swing, and try to hit it.

If you do, the clubface will strike the ball exactly where it is supposed to be hit.

54 Hard Underfoot

The most powerful swings are made by coiling the body around the inside of the right leg.

This move is not so easy to pull off. Many golfers find themselves concentrating so much on the inside of the leg that they end up executing what is termed a reverse-C. They sway to the *left* on the backswing and to the right on the downswing—a move that removes all power and precision from the golf swing.

Here's a drill to help you get a feel for the correct coil: When you take your stance, put a golf ball under your right foot, just in front of the heel. Swing normally. You'll notice that you cannot move your weight to the right because to do so would mean shifting it to the outside of your right foot, and you can't do that because the golf ball is there. What the ball does is effectively transfer the weight up the inside of your leg.

A secondary benefit of this drill is that it teaches you to "fire" the right side—that is, to make the right side of the body add extra power to the swing, a move that most of the top pros make but one that most amateurs find difficult to control.

55 Knuckle Up

Here's a rundown of the three main hand positions golfers adopt at the top of the swing.

When the left hand is under the right hand, that's called open because this position opens the face of the golf club. When the left wrist is bent toward the back of the head, the hands are said to be "closed" because the clubface is closed. Neither position is ideal.

The ideal position has the hands square, with the clubface square, and a very good way to achieve this is to concentrate on having your knuckles point straight up to the sky when you reach the top of your swing.

If you concentrate on extending your left knuckles away and up to the top of the backswing, they should reach the top pointing straight up.

56 Divot Education

You can tell quite a lot from the divot (turf dug up by your club at impact). Here's a primer:

• The Fat Divot. The fat divot begins an inch or so behind the ball. You probably swayed too far to the right on your backswing and didn't get your weight back over to the left on the downswing. Or, perhaps, you tried to hit the ball too hard and lowered your right shoulder as you began your downswing. Either way, your ball probably hasn't traveled very far.

• The Divot That Points to the Right. If your divot hole "points" right of your target after you've hit, you're swinging from the inside to the outside at impact and have probably hooked the ball. You're perhaps addressing the ball with a closed stance or swinging on too flat a plane.

• The Divot That Points to the Left. The opposite of the above. Now you're swinging from outside to in, and you've probably sliced the ball. Check your address position. If the fault isn't there, it's likely that you're swinging with your hands and arms and pulling the club across the ball instead of allowing your lower body to lead the swing along the target line.

• No Divot at All. Unless you're hitting from a tee or putting, you're not hitting down and through. As the idea is to let the grooves of the club and the aerodynamics of the dimpled ball get the ball airborne, you *should* take a divot (and replace it when you've hit). It could be that you're raising your body as you swing back, or perhaps your ball position is too far to the left. You can cure the former by concentrating on turning your shoulders as you swing back, and solve the latter by moving the ball to the right at address. How far to the right? Simple: until you start taking divots that begin right behind the ball.

57 Turf Technique

At some point in your golfing life, you may get a chance to play on a "links" golf course. Such courses are to be found by the sea—on land that *was* the sea and is said today to "link" the mainland with it—and are prevalent along the coasts of Scotland and Ireland.

Links courses are known for being treeless and windy, so the shots we discuss in the chapter on trouble play should put you in good stead. But the biggest difference from a ball-striking point of view is the turf.

The ground on a links course is sandy and very firm. The grass is fescue, a tight, curly grass that is also very hardy. It's a wonderful surface from which to hit a golf ball, but some adjustments do have to be made.

• You must anticipate more roll than normal. If you usually hit 240 yards from the tee, figure on 260 on a links course.

• On long- and middle-iron shots, it's best to play the ball an inch or two farther back in your stance. This means you'll make a more descending blow. Your ball will really zip.

• Don't be too quick to pull out your sand wedge for fairway shots. The ground tends to be too tight to allow the flange to get under the club (it bounces), and approach shots on these courses should be of the "bounce-and-run" variety. A sand wedge is for target golf.

58 Going Too Far

Swing keys are wonderful until you start going overboard. Let's say you keep forgetting to position your hands just ahead of the ball at impact. You work on it and work on it, then before you know it your hands are so far ahead that the clubface is closed and you're smothering every shot you hit.

If you fall prey to this bad habit, you're not alone. All golfers do to some extent. There are golfers out there who have been bedeviled with a hook all their lives, then work so long and so hard on changing their address, grip, and swing plane that soon they're stuck with a slice.

About the only thing you can do is to check your basics regularly—weekly if you play only at weekends, every few days if you play daily. Ben Crenshaw used to keep a list of the swing keys that worked for him. You should do this, too, because then you'll have a record of some of the keys you've been *overdoing.*

59 Don't Bite

The golfer who faces a long-iron shot to his target is bound to be nervous, particularly if he has an area of trouble to carry. But, while the shot won't get any easier, the golfer can give himself a better chance of hitting the ball well by relaxing. He should first take a few deep breaths before swinging and then relax his *jaws.*

Now before you laugh, try clenching your teeth—as 99.9 percent of golfers do over most shots—and then unclench them. Do you notice how this relaxes not only the jaw but the entire upper-body area as well?

A fan sent this simple tip to Jack Nicklaus several years ago, and he tried it immediately. The funny thing is that if there is one person in this universe who doesn't need help hitting the toughest shots, it's Nicklaus.

But the rest of us? The more we unclench, the better.

60 A Balancing Act

To achieve both good balance during the swing and a good weight shift, think of the insides of your feet and legs as "balance points."

When your weight shifts to your right side, as it should do during the backswing, have the inside of your right foot and leg bear that weight. Then, when your weight has to shift to your left side, think of the inside of your left foot and leg taking the weight. (Note that you can't do this throughout the swing, as you'll finish your follow-through with your weight on the outside of your left foot.)

Finally, a good way to start with your weight in the proper place is to address the ball with your knees pointed in slightly. But don't bend the knees in too much or you won't be able to move at all.

61 Stomach It

Where should the full swing finish? It's a valid question, because many golfers either cut the swing short and block the ball to the right or swing too hard and end up off balance.

And the answer is a simple one: Finish the swing when your stomach is pointing at the target.

Try it a few times. Don't think about hitting the ball, your swing plane, or anything else. Just swing the club easily, and gradually you'll get a feel for the perfect follow-through.

62 Eye It—or Not?

"Keep your eye on the ball" is the oldest piece of advice in the game—and not a bad piece, at that—but it's possible to get so wrapped up in looking at the ball that you end up staring at it and forgetting what you're there to do, that is, to hit the ball at the target.

Instead, you should look at the ball and then start thinking about the shape of the shot you're trying to hit. Visualize it flying toward its target. That way you'll avoid any obsession with staring at the ball.

63 Got a Loop?

Ben Crenshaw once said of Miller Barber's swing that Barber looked as though he were getting the club caught on a clothesline.

Raymond Floyd fans the clubhead—he opens it by moving his right hand under his left—very early on the backswing and loops it into position at the top of the swing.

Lee Trevino does the opposite. He takes the clubhead back outside the target line and loops it back in.

What all these golfers have in common is that they've been very successful—and they get themselves into perfect position at the point of impact.

The message here is clear: If you do have a funky backswing, don't worry too much. Work on the impact position.

64 In Reverse Order

The backswing contains five moving parts, and there is a proper sequence to those movements. So it stands to reason that the downswing should also have five moving parts, and that they should move, for all intents and purposes, in reverse.

The order of movement for the backswing is as follows: hands, arms, shoulders, hips, legs. (Although you'll hear that the hands, arms, and shoulders start their moves together, there is no question that the hands have to move farther than the shoulders and should therefore be given priority.)

On the downswing, think in reverse order: Legs, hips, shoulders, arms, hands. That will help you uncoil into a controlled and powerful hit.

65 More Imagery for the Top

To avoid hitting from the top—beginning your downswing before you've properly completed your backswing—imagine yourself "laying" the club on a delicate surface when you are at the top of the backswing.

The idea here is to prevent the hands and arms from jerking the club, so try to hold the club as loosely as possible at the top of the swing. Imagine yourself laying the club on a tray of eggs without breaking them. Other popular images are a bed of feathers and a soft pillow.

But whatever you imagine, make sure it is something that suggests softness, because the whole point of the exercise to to loosen and lighten your grip—to take the grip out of play.

66 A Double Take

One of the simplest ways to take all the complexity out of the golf swing is to think of your address position as the impact position as well. All you have to do then is program your mind and body to remember your address position, swing the club back, and return to your original position as you hit.

This is also a good way to ensure a sound address. If, for instance, you feel funny standing over the ball—your hands may be way behind the ball, or the ball may be in the wrong position—then why do you think you'll feel comfortable at impact?

67 The No-Sweep Sweep

When you hit fairway woods or long irons, the idea is to sweep the ball off the ground, scuffing the grass but not taking a divot.

Would that this sweep shot were so easy.

It's natural for a golfer to want to hit down behind the ball. When a ball isn't teed up, the optimum point of contact is just before the bottom of the swing. But when you make contact and also try to sweep, you're likely to hold the club back and hit the ball thin.

This doesn't make a lot of sense. Just like other irons, fairway woods and long irons should be hit with a descending blow (although not *that* descending). Leave the grooves on the clubface and the dimples on the ball to do the necessary aerodynamic work.

Forget about trying to sweep. Hit down and through your ball and you'll do just fine.

68 Working Six to Twelve

To get a better mental picture of the swing planes used in a straight shot, a draw (right to left), and a fade (left to right), think of yourself standing on the face of a huge clock, with the ball at the center of the dial and the target line running from six o'clock—to your right—to twelve o'clock.

If you were to address the ball and hit a straight shot, you would swing back to six o'clock and then through to twelve. For a fade, you would swing from five o'clock to eleven o'clock. For a draw, you would swing from seven o'clock out to one o'clock.

If you tend to make the same mistake consistently, this imagery can help you. In other words, if you tend to slice the ball, think in terms of swinging from seven to one. The hookers among us should swing from five to eleven. You'll straighten out pretty quickly.

69 The Three L's

You've heard of the three R's: reading, 'riting, and 'rithmetic. Well, the golf swing has the three L's. They're to be found halfway into the backswing, at the top of the swing, and just before impact.

1. Halfway into your backswing your arms should be roughly parallel to the ground, your wrists cocked, and the club pointing vertically up into the air. The angle formed by the club and your arms is the first L.

2. At the top of your swing your arms should be roughly vertical and the club should be horizontal, parallel to the ground. This forms the second L.

3. Just before impact your arms will be pointing just to the right of the ball, your wrists should still be fully cocked, and your club should stick out at right angles to your arms. This is your third L, and the toughest to form.

If you think of making these three L's during the swing, you'll soon develop power and strength in your swing.

70 A Good Pointer

You can keep your club on a good, upright swing plane by making sure the grip end of the shaft points directly at your target halfway into your backswing.

Were you to take the club too far outside the target line on your backswing—a slice swing, in other words—the grip end would point somewhere around your left thigh. Take it back too far inside the target line—a hook swing—and the grip end would be pointing away from you.

When the club points at the target, however, you will be "on plane" and in a good position to make a full turn and hit a powerful shot.

71 Free the Mind

Never take too many swing keys onto the golf course. You'll confuse the mind rather than free it up to play good golf.

What you choose may depend on the circumstances. If you've seen a recent improvement in a particular part of your game, you may want to focus on maintaining that improvement. You may choose a swing key based on how a particular course plays. If it's a course with small greens and tough greenside rough, you may want to remember a swing key that helps your short game (the theory being that you're going to miss a green or two). And if the weather is windy, you may want to focus on swinging within yourself and keeping the ball low.

One thing you cannot do is maintain

the improvement in your game, focus on your short game, swing within yourself, *and* keep the ball low. It's just too much for one golfing mind.

72 Manual Logic

Almost every shot in the game should be struck with the hands ahead of the ball. Why this is so could well be the subject of a scientific dissertation.

We prefer to recall the old joke about the man who is spotted pulling a piece of string down the street when a friend stops him.

"Why are you pulling a piece of string?" the friend asks.

"Have you ever tried *pushing* one?" the man replies.

The principle in golf is the same. The hands stay ahead, so they in effect pull the club through the swing. It's a lot easier—and more effective—than pushing it.

73 Cross Them Up

When you hit a ball thin, there's a good chance that you didn't incorporate good arm and hand action in your swing.

It's true that swinging *with* the hands and arms is not advisable—you would likely hit a weak shot off to the left—but the arms and hands do play their part in solid shot making.

Here's a drill to help you understand how: Hit shots with your legs crossed. It really doesn't matter which leg crosses over which. Once they're crossed, take a middle or long iron and start hitting balls. You won't be able to make a full backswing because your hips can't turn, but you will be able to achieve a full (or close to full) follow-through.

Once you combine this new feeling with good leg action, you will truly have a full swing.

74 Limited Weight

The fairway woods should be hit with a little more control than you would use when hitting a driver. That's because, while it makes sense to hit for a specific spot with your driver, you'll often use a fairway wood for an approach shot, and golf shots don't come more specific than that.

While you should still make a full shoulder turn, you can keep this club under control by limiting the weight shift to your right side during the backswing. (If you think about it, it's the first step in a progression toward the short clubs in which less weight is shifted right; by the time you get short chips, almost all your weight is on your left side.)

You'll find that this encourages a tighter turn and eliminates sway. You then can uncoil into a full, controlled shot.

75 Left-Thumb Hike

We talk elsewhere about "shaking" an imaginary hand with your own right hand to make sure that your right hand is in the correct position during the backswing. Here's a drill for the left hand that will give you a good feel of left hand movement during the downswing:

Imagine you're a hitchhiker—and not a very lucky one. Cars pass from your right and you stick out your left thumb. As they pass by, you let your upraised thumb follow the car, and as they disappear into the distance you hold your thumb out in one last desperate effort to make the drivers see you.

The left-hand action in the golf swing is very similar. Try hitching a lift a few times, and then try it with a club in your left hand only, the thumb down the shaft (or "up" in this case). By the end of the swing you'll have full extension of the left arm down the target line.

76 Polar Opposites

If you suffer from a slice or a hook, the best way to get rid of it is to hit the opposite shot deliberately.

- *Slicers.* Learn the principles of the hooked shot: the strong grip (right hand almost under the grip), the closed stance, the closed clubface, and the inside-to-out swing plane. Now try your best to hit a hook.

- *Hookers.* Learn the principles of the slice: the weak grip (right hand almost on top of the grip), the open stance, the open club face, and the outside-to-in swing.

We're not advocating that you swap one fault for another. But knowing the elements of their opposites will help you understand your existing faults and make you a better all-round player.

77 Driver from the Deck

There will be occasions when it is possible to take the "big dog" out and let it loose from the fairway. The key, however, is (as always) the lie.

Never hit the driver from a tight lie. Generally there just isn't enough loft to get the ball airborne. If the clubface can make contact with the *lower* half of the ball, however, then you're in business.

Swing as you would with a fairway wood: Minimize your leg action, don't shift your weight as much to the left as you would with a teed shot, and hit down and through (but not as much as you would with an iron).

Two final tips: If the grain of the grass is growing toward your ball, don't hit the driver; it will get snagged. And if you carry a metal driver, you'll be in even better shape, because metal woods get the ball airborne more easily than wooden ones.

78 The Same Old Angle

One way to stop swaying during the golf swing is to keep the right leg anchored throughout the swing.

The wrong way to do this is to tighten the leg muscles and "grip" the ground. It's just not necessary.

It's a better idea to check the angle between your right leg and the ground to the right of your stance. It's probably a little over ninety degrees. All you have to do is focus on maintaining that angle, and you should perform a good coil around your right side that will lead to a strong, powerful swing.

79 Copycat

One way to learn a good golf swing is to choose the swing of a great player and copy it. The only way you can do this effectively is to get your hands on either an instructional tape or a tournament tape. But that's quite easy these days.

Make sure that you choose one swing, and stick with one swing. You can't play like Nick Faldo one day and like Tom Kite the next. That just breeds inconsistency and confusion.

FIVE

Driving Lessons

80 Pull Through

There's always a tendency to uncock the wrists early on the downswing in an effort to unleash a little more energy into the hit. But this action causes the wrists to break, and you're likely either to top your ball, blade it, or snap-hook it.

You can avoid this by deliberately pulling the club down into the back of your ball with your left hand. Don't worry about smothering the ball. As your weight shifts to your left side and the body opens up, you'll find that the club uncocks naturally.

81 Hip Power

You'll generate a lot of power if you forget about building up the muscles in your body and concentrate instead on whipping the hips.

Look at Gary Player. He's only five feet seven inches tall, but he hits the ball a long way by moving his hips as fast as possible from right to left in the downswing.

But not so fast that he loses control of the swing. The idea is to have the hips moving to the left, where they'll open naturally. If you keep your head behind the ball through impact, you'll form a sort of human catapult that will send your ball soaring.

82 The Other Ball

Jack Nicklaus has often said that one of his swing keys is to keep his clubhead traveling along the target line (an imaginary straight line between ball and target) as long as possible.

It's a good thought, because it helps you extend through the ball on the follow-through instead of "quitting" at impact—that is, not completing the follow-through.

To keep the clubhead down the target line, imagine the target line extending toward your target and then focus on keeping the clubhead traveling along that line.

83 The Double-Ball Trick

Another way to keep the clubhead traveling down the target line after impact is to think of yourself as hitting *two* balls. Imagine a ball is positioned about eighteen inches to two feet to the left of the actual ball. After you hit the real ball, hit the imaginary ball as well, and to do that, you must have a full extension on the follow-through.

84 Ironing Day

These three key factors may persuade you to hit an iron instead of a driver from the tee:

1. the design of the hole
2. the weather
3. the state of your golf swing

"Design" refers to the breadth of the fairway, the length of the hole, and sometimes the direction of the hole. If the fairway is narrow, an iron should give you a better chance of hitting it (a fairway wood's not a bad choice either, in this instance). If the hole is short, and you don't need maximum distance from the tee to give you a short iron to the green, go for the iron. In fact, unless you can drive the green, ideally you want to be between 75 and 100 yards back, as that will allow you a full wedge shot. Last, if the hole doglegs to the left or right at a point where a well-hit drive would travel *through* the turn and into the rough beyond, then you should take just enough club to reach the turn—an iron, in other words.

It's a good idea to use an iron in windy weather simply because it's an easier club to control. Control is more important than distance in any weather—but especially in the windy stuff.

If you're not making solid contact, or are spraying the ball with the driver, go with an iron. Once you regain your confidence, work back to the driver.

85 Choke Down

One option for better accuracy on tight holes is to choke down a few inches on the grip of the driver. A shorter, firmer swing will enhance accuracy without sacrificing too much distance (you'll still hit longer than you would with a fairway wood).

The key here is to cut down on the wrist cock and make a three-quarter swing. In other words, you shouldn't really give yourself an opportunity to hit an off-line drive.

86 Three Pics to Click

Your driving will improve if, before you swing, you draw a mental picture of:

1. your position at the top of your swing

2. the clubhead swinging through the impact area

3. where you want your club to finish up (the best way to do this is to pick out a target on the horizon and swing your club toward it)

These images represent the three keys to any good swing: the backswing, the impact, and the follow-through.

87 Stay Up

Always club down from a driver if, in so doing, you avoid a downhill lie for your second shot.

The downhill lie is the toughest of all lies to hit from. An uphill lie, though, isn't difficult at all, just so long as your club selection compensates for the slope. A flat lie is by far the best lie to hit from.

So if by staying away from your driver you have the option of a flat or an uphill lie—don't think twice. Club down.

88 Up, Up, and Away

One way to hit the ball higher when driving—an especially useful strategy when the wind is behind you—is to make sure you hit the lower half of the ball.

You can do this by teeing the ball at the normal height—half the ball lies above the top of the clubface—then concentrating on hitting the tee out of the ground.

You won't miss the ball, because there's just not enough room for the driver to pass through underneath it. And you shouldn't hit the ground either, because the only way you can knock the tee out of the ground is to hit the top of it.

SIX

Iron Play

A Knockout Punch

You'll find the punch shot especially useful when you're playing into the wind. You can also play this shot in other situations, such as when you want to hit under a tree limb.

It's not a difficult shot to learn, and the key is to stay low throughout the swing.

Play the ball farther back in your stance so that you hit down into the back of the ball and put a lot of spin on it. As you address the ball, put more of your weight on your left side. Make your normal backswing, but as you swing down and through the ball, focus on driving low through the ball—your weight still mostly on your left side—and finish your swing with the club in a low position.

You can employ variations on the same theme for other shots. For instance, if you want to hit a low shot that runs up and onto the green, play much the same shot, but hit the ball more softly so that it doesn't travel so far and spins less (and therefore runs more).

90 Don't Press Your Long Irons

The forward press (a slight forward movement of the hands) sets the hands ahead of the ball—the ideal position at impact—early in the swing and gets you into a rhythm just as the ball is about to be hit.

Elsewhere we warn not to press too far. With the long irons, however, you shouldn't press at all.

Think about it: Many of us don't hit a 1- or a 2-iron because they're too difficult to hit and use effectively. Neither club has enough loft for us to get the ball up and into the air. So why would you press a 3-iron and turn it into a 2-iron?

Pressing long irons raises the possibility of a smothered shot—the action makes a risky shot even riskier.

91 Flying High

Rule number one for hitting a high iron shot is: Never use your body to try to lift the ball. Your swing, the loft and grooves of the club, and the dimples of the ball should do the work.

But here's a tip to help you get in a position to swing properly: Keep your weight back on your right side when you hit a high shot (it's the opposite of putting more weight on your left side to hit a low punch shot). But don't fall into the trap of swaying to the right.

An easy way of keeping your weight back is to widen your stance: Take your normal address position and then move your right foot farther to the right.

Don't move your left foot; it's fine where it is. Moving the right foot will automatically keep your weight behind the ball.

92 Wind Selection

When selecting irons on a windy day, remember these two keys:

1. When hitting *into* the wind, your ball will stop almost immediately, so plan to have your approaches land as close to the hole as possible.

2. When hitting *with* the wind, choose the club that, in normal conditions, would land your ball just in front of the green. Usually the wind will carry the ball onto the green, but even if you come up short, there is a very good chance that the wind will cause your ball to bounce and roll onto the green.

93 Hitting into the Wind

You will hear lots of tips about hitting into wind: how you should finish low to hit a low shot, how you should keep your hands ahead of the ball, and so on. They're all good tips (and some are included in this book), but here's a mental tip that may be the soundest advice of all:

When you're hitting into the wind, don't swing harder. Swing *better.*

There is a terrific temptation to swipe with all one's might when faced with a stiff wind. Golfers who do this swing off balance, make a dreadful weight shift, and have little or no chance of making solid contact.

Swinging better means forgetting about hitting harder. Concentrate instead on gaining much-needed distance by doing all the things that promote firm, solid contact with the ball. Contact is far more important than brute strength when you're hitting a golf ball—even more so in the wind.

94 Club up the Slope

Remember that when you face an uphill shot to a green, you'll need more club than you would hit on a shot to a green at fairway level.

How many clubs you should go up depends on how high the green is raised, and also on wind direction. But unless there is out-of-bounds or similarly drastic trouble behind the green, it's always better to err on the long side.

The same applies for shots hit downhill, but here it's best to err on the short side. That's because shots hit downhill tend to be shorter than they look, and even if you do come up short, it's possible that the slope will carry your ball onto or close to the green.

95 Play It Straight

Always hit your short irons dead straight.

The straightest golf shot is the toughest to hit—that's why pros consistently hit from left to right or vice versa—so this may seem like bad advice. But the point is that because the shorter irons are actually shorter in length, it's easier for you to return the club face square to the ball at impact.

You're ahead of the game, in other words, so trying to curve a ball on a particular trajectory just complicates the process.

When hitting with short irons, step up to your ball, imagine a straight line to the hole, and then hit the ball straight down that line.

96 At Dawn's Early Light

The greens at most golf courses are watered at sundown, during the night, and at first light. This means that if you are playing earlier in the day, you will be hitting approach shots to well-watered greens.

And what *this* means is that you can be more aggressive with your approaches. Your ball is much more likely to hold the green.

Ask any top player when he scores best and he'll say right after rainfall—for exactly the same reason.

97 Hit to the Flag

At some point when calculating your yardage from the green, you will probably ask whether the yardage is to the center of the green or to the front.

But how often do you then calculate according to whether the flag is positioned in the front, the middle, or the back?

Some courses make this easy for you, attaching a smaller flag to the top (for back position), middle (for middle position) or bottom (for front position).

Remember, there could be a significant difference in yardage between a front and a back position, perhaps up to two or three clubs. So don't just get your yardage to the middle of the green and hit the corresponding club. Go the extra yard and get the exact yardage.

98 Background Rules

When judging distance, take into consideration what's behind the green as well as the position of the green itself.

The background can create an optical illusion. If the green is surrounded by trees, it likely will appear closer than it actually is. If you're playing a flattish, treeless course, and there is no background to speak of, then the green will look to be farther away than it really is. (It's also tougher to get a mental picture of approaches to open area; that's why tournament players find it easier to hit at greens surrounded by galleries.)

So if you have doubts about a hole's yardage, take note of the background before you make your club selection.

99 Late-Season Roll

An approach shot that requires a 5-iron in spring may require only a 6- or a 7-iron in the fall. That's because late in the year you have to play a whole new ball game.

As the golf season progresses—obviously, this doesn't apply where golf is played year-round—your golf course changes. Because the days become shorter and cooler in the fall, the fairways need less water and so they become less lush and much faster. In addition, after all the golf that has been played, the ground tends to become more compact and gives even more roll.

The same applies to greens. They become firmer and tougher to hold. Generally, these conditions make you a little longer off the tee, while also forcing you to hit some approaches short of the green and allow them to roll to the target area.

The game now becomes less a game of target golf and more a game of *creative* golf. For this reason, many golfers consider the fall the very best time to play.

100 Don't Be Fooled

Let's say you face an approach shot to a green that slopes steeply downward from right to left, with a bunker guarding the front left and no trouble at all on the right. Where do you aim?

If you answer, "To the right, away from the trouble," then you are wrong. Or rather, you haven't taken the slope of the green into consideration.

If you miss your approach, you'll face a chip down the slope—and it will be almost impossible to hold the green. Count yourself lucky if you take four shots to get down from where you were in the fairway.

Now, let's say you miss to the left; you hit into that dreaded bunker. You face a sand shot back up the slope—not that tough a shot. If you come up short from the sand—as most golfers do—you'll have an uphill putt.

The point is this: Good golf-course architects set out to *deceive* the golfer, and often a hazard will make you play your approach toward a far more difficult position. You can avoid this by weighing the risks of your next shot and remembering that such hazards as bunkers are not necessarily where the trouble lies.

101 Don't Cock Early

When you're hitting short-iron shots, don't cock your wrists too early.

Many golfers cock their wrists early in the swing because when they see top players they *appear* to be doing just that. But it's an optical illusion caused by the length of the short iron. As the swing arc is shorter, the wrists cock in less time.

The point is that the motion of the swing should determine when the wrists are cocked, and problems arise when golfers mistake this natural cocking for a deliberate movement and begin to pick up the club at the start of the swing.

No matter what club you are hitting, draw it back from the ball low to the ground and let the wrists cock naturally as the club comes up and around your body.

Start your short-iron swings as you would your long ones: low and slow.

102 Mix and Match

Here's a handy way of choosing where to hit for on a green:

Most greens have four pin positions: very easy, easy, difficult, and very difficult. If you play a particular course regularly, you'll soon learn which is which (if you don't already know).

Assign each pin position a number according to its difficulty, from "1" for very easy to "4" for very difficult.

Before playing a round, go to the practice range and rank yourself according to how well you strike the ball. If you're swinging badly and making poor contact—we all have those days—assign yourself a "1." If you've never struck the ball better, give yourself a "4."

Put the numbers together when you play. If you're playing at level "2," do not try to hit at a pin that is a "3" or a "4." If you do merit a "4," then go for everything.

In other words, don't hit at pins you're not skilled enough to reach.

103 Know Your Numbers

It is said that players should measure the average distance they hit all their irons. That's true, but if you can at least get an accurate handle on how far you hit every club from the 7-iron to the finesse (or third) wedge, then you'll be well ahead of the game.

But even that's not enough to really know your short irons. You should get to know your yardage:

- with a smooth swing, the club grounded normally
- with a hard swing, the club grounded normally
- with a smooth swing, the club hooded (delofted) slightly
- with a hard swing, the club hooded slightly.

Let's say you can work out these yardages for the 7-, 8-, and 9-irons and for the pitching, sand, and third wedges. You now have twenty-four yardages and twenty-four different shots. Your arsenal of scoring shots has suddenly become much bigger.

104 What's the Slot?

When advanced golfers discuss short-iron play, they often talk about dropping the club into a "slot" on the downswing. Here's what they mean:

When they reach the end of their backswing—with short irons this generally does not mean a full backswing to the parallel position—their wrists are not fully cocked. But as they begin their downswing, they tuck the right elbow closer to the body and drop the hands straight down. This action cocks the wrists, forming a ninety-degree angle between arms and club—and builds power. As they reach impact, the wrists uncock and the golfers hit down and through.

Dropping the club into the slot really is a power move for the advanced golfer, but it's not a difficult technique to learn.

105 A Little Extra Spin

When you want your ball to stop quickly on the green, you should play it slightly farther back in your stance so that you hit earlier in your swing arc with a more downward blow.

Beware, however, that playing farther

back effectively delofts the clubface slightly, which could mean extra distance. You won't want to compensate by swinging easier—that takes away the spin you're trying to obtain—but you can choke down on the grip slightly or choose a more lofted club.

106 The Laws of Low

Hitting a low shot is not just a matter of hooding the club face. You'll also want to play the ball back in your stance and choke down on the club.

When you play the ball back in your stance, it is important to remember that you should not just move your feet to the left. This forces you to come into the ball at a much steeper angle and you could well hit the shot fat. It's better to take your normal stance and then widen it slightly by moving *the left foot only* to the left. You will want a slightly more descending blow; so when you move your left foot, also shift your weight to your left side and move your hands forward.

As for choking down on the grip, the idea is not necessarily to give you more control over the club. Gripping farther down the shaft effectively shortens the area in which the shaft can flex, so the shaft becomes a little stiffer. That will make your ball fly lower too.

But choking down will lose you some distance, so take one more club than you usually would for that distance.

SEVEN

Greenside Play

107 Read Chips Too

Why is it that a golfer who will spend an endless—and unnecessary—amount of time reading a putt from every direction on the compass won't even take a second look at the line of a chip?

You should, because the best chips get the ball rolling as fast as possible. And while you're far less likely to hole a chip than a putt, you can't expect to get a chip close unless you first get an idea of the grain, the break, the undulations of the green, and the expected speed of the green.

So take time to line up a chip as you would a putt—quickly but conclusively. And then hit it.

108 Know Your Grain

Knowing the effect the grain of the green will have on your ball when you're chipping or pitching is just as important as knowing how the grain will affect a putt.

Let's say you're chipping against the grain (the grass is growing toward you). When your ball first hits the ground, it will run into this grass "wall" and stop quickly. You can compensate for this two ways:

1. by lofting the ball closer to the hole and anticipating that it will stop quickly

2. by taking a less-lofted club and rolling the ball *firmly* toward the hole.

Now let's say you're chipping with the grain running away from you, or down-grain. Your ball is more likely to skip off the top of the grass and bounce and roll. To make sure you don't zip past the hole:

- Don't hit your ball as hard as you would against the grain.
- Use a more lofted club (although this is not a good idea if you have a bad lie).

109 Cross Yourself Up

Some golfers change their putting grips from regular to cross-handed to ensure that their hands remain quiet and their wrists firm throughout their swing.

Only one other commonly played

shot requires the same firm wrists, and that is a chip. So is it unreasonable to use a cross-handed grip when chipping?

Unreasonable, no. Unheard of, yes. The grip may take some getting used to, but it is effective—especially for those who find themselves hitting chips fat or blading them. A leading cause of poor chipping is allowing the wrists to be involved to the point that they prevent solid contact. A cross-handed grip may remedy that.

110 Roll from the Rough Stuff

When you want to roll your ball on the green from a greenside lie, and the ball lies in rough that is too tough to get a middle iron on, your best bet is to take a more lofted club and hook it.

The idea is to impart topspin on the ball to make it roll farther than it normally would, and thereby compensate for the loft on the club.

Address your ball, then close the blade, swing inside the target line slightly, and flip the wrists slightly counterclockwise at impact. (Just don't let the right hand get too active or you might close the blade completely and smother the ball.)

Your ball will pop out of the rough

and start rolling briskly toward its target.

111 Chip Close

When you face a short chip that you intend to strike much as you would a putt, do what you should also do with a putt: Play the ball closer to your body. This positions your eyes over the intended line—allowing you to read breaks and rolls much more effectively—and also helps you swing the club straight back and through. When the ball is farther from your feet, you may have a tendency to swing inside-out, or vice versa, and push or pull the chip.

Just play the ball closer to your body—position it off your right toe, keep your hands ahead, and swing firmly back and through.

112 Near No-Hitter

When you face a delicate chip shot from greenside rough and want your ball to pop up softly and settle—to a tight position or on a downhill slope—you'll want to all but *miss* your ball.

This is one of the few shots in golf in which you hit with your hands slightly *behind* the ball at address. Your stance should be open, your weight should be on your left side, and the ball should be played forward.

Take the club—a pitching wedge is best—back as far as you can without breaking your wrists and then swing forward. The idea is to just pass the club under the ball, barely nudging it. The ball still will jump up, but as you haven't put any "hit" in it, it won't spin, nor will it roll much on landing.

113 One Bounce Is Enough

When you face a delicate downhill shot from greenside rough to a putting surface that slopes away from you, you should use the rough to put the brakes on your ball.

The idea is to bounce the ball once in the rough, let the longer grass slow it down, and then hope that the ball doesn't roll too far past the hole.

The shot should be played like any other chip from greenside rough: lofted club, hands forward, ball off right foot, upright swing, and then a firm hit.

You do not want to get too clever with this shot by playing the hands back to take away some of its power and slow it even more. This action could lead to the ball bouncing in the rough and then not having enough momentum to reach the green.

And that's key here: Make sure your ball bounces only *once* before it hits the putting surface. If it bounces twice, it won't go much farther and then you'll face *another* delicate shot from greenside rough to a downhill putting surface.

Don't worry if your ball does roll past the hole after bouncing once. The chances of getting within tap-in distance are almost nil in such situations and at least you'll be putting—and putting back uphill.

114 When the Exception Is the Rule

When you hit your ball into rough, you will want to take the most lofted club and escape as quickly and as easily as possible, correct?

Not always. When you're in rough around the green, you may want to use a *less* lofted club, because it will help you avoid skulling your ball—that is, hitting the fat of the ball with the leading edge of your club.

The leading edge of a lofted club like a sand wedge is designed to pass under the ball to help you get it up into the air. But for this to happen your ball must be sitting up in grass, or in sand.

If your ball is in a tight lie—say, in greenside rough—and you use a lofted club, the leading edge can easily bounce off the ground behind the ball and rebound *into* the ball, sending it flying hard and low across the green.

In these situations, the best thing you can do is take a middle iron—a 5- or a 6-, perhaps—and *concentrate on hitting the ball first.* Then it's just a matter of working out the line, the grain, and the break.

115 Poorer Means Farther Back

The rule of thumb for hitting chips and pitches from beside the green is: The worse the lie, the farther back in your stance you play the ball.

It's tougher to make good contact when your ball is in a bad lie, and playing it farther back means you'll get to the ball earlier in your swing arc, before any rough gets a chance to interfere with the club head.

116 What You Leave Is What You Get

Pro golfers hate playing pro-ams with amateur partners who walk around the hole. The amateurs are careful not to walk on the pros' lines, but they never think twice about walking *behind* the hole.

This drives the pros bananas because they figure that if they miss—and they expect to miss their share—then their next putt likely will be a comebacker from the area the amateurs are digging up with their spikes!

Here again you should think a shot or two ahead—in this case, to ensure as many smooth putts as possible.

This is a lesson you should also bear in mind when you're chipping. The idea, though, is not to leave a putt that's bereft of spike marks (although that would be desirable). Rather, you want to try to leave yourself with *the putt you're most likely to hole*, and thinking ahead will help you do this. As most golfers want a putt that's straight uphill, you should try to leave your chips below the hole.

117 The No-Risk Chip

When you hit short chips around the green, you should make pure and solid contact with the ball. Without that, your ability to read the line or choose the best club is all for naught.

Here are four quick tips to help you achieve solid contact:

1. *Keep your weight on your left foot,* as shifting your weight during the chip could easily lead you to hit the ball thin or fat.

2. Open your stance and *play the ball opposite your right foot.*

3. Start the chip with your *hands opposite the inside of your left thigh,* and keep them ahead of the ball at impact.

4. *Keep your wrists firm throughout the chip,* using your arms and shoulders as a pendulum, much as you should do when you putt.

118 Sit on It

When hitting short irons, you stand closer to the ball than you do with any other club (except perhaps the putter). Yet it's amazing how many golfers don't know exactly how far to stand from the ball.

If you stand too far away, you'll very likely commit a roundhouse swing and yank the ball to the left. If you stand too close to the ball, you'll come into it too steeply and likely will hit behind it.

The correct way to determine how far to stand from the ball, therefore, is to pretend that you're about to sit on a low wall while keeping your weight evenly distributed from the front to the back of your feet, and with more weight on your left side than your right.

Now put the club head on the ground. *That* is your ideal stance.

119 Do It the Hard Way

With all the walking that goes on around the green, it's no surprise—especially in late summer—that hardpan becomes, in effect, an extra hazard on the course.

It's tough to hit a soft, high shot from hardpan, but most golfers don't even give themselves a chance. They try to scoop up the ball by breaking the wrists before impact and end up topping it or blading it.

If ever there was a case for letting the club do the work, this is it. Simply keep your wrists and hands out of the swing by concentrating on keeping the hands ahead of the ball at impact.

You may at first find yourself firing hot little chips at the pin, but in time you'll get a feel for gripping and swinging softly.

120 He Popped It Up!

The little pop shot is handy to know for those times when you have little green to work with. But as it's a precision shot, you should practice before taking it out on the golf course.

The idea is to pop the ball up sharply and land it with little or no roll. Take a lofted club—a sand or a pitching wedge—open your stance (move your left foot back from the target line), and play the ball opposite your left foot with the clubface slightly open. With the weight on your left side, swing back outside the line.

Now here's the key maneuver: You'll want to break your wrists sharply on the backswing, and then swing down and through *with your wrists still cocked.* Think of pulling the clubhead through with your left hand and you should be fine.

Try to hit the back of the ball and the ground at the same time, making contact before you reach the bottom of your downswing and being sure to follow through.

Because you're swinging down from outside the line with your clubface open—a slice shot, in effect—the ball is likely to jump to the right when it lands, much like a bunker shot, so you should aim to the left to compensate.

121 To Spot or Not?

It's a good idea to aim for a particular spot when you're chipping (in much the same way that you try to hit over a certain spot when putting). You should work out where you'll need to land the ball to get it rolling to the hole, and then concentrate only on landing your ball on that spot.

But don't concentrate too hard. Or, rather, don't let your desire to hit the spot take precedence over your desire to get the ball close to the hole. A lot of golfers find their spot, hit their shot, and then look up quickly to see if they actually hit it.

Why they do this is anybody's guess. It could be that they're eager to see if they calculated correctly, or maybe hitting the spot at least mitigates the miscalculated shot—as in, "Well, at least I hit it where I wanted it. It just took off on me."

Whatever the reason, the chances are that the golfer who looks up to see if he's hit the spot will miss it. You can't do two things at once.

122 The Early Cock

On certain delicate shots around the green you'll be required to cock the wrists early and hit sharply down into the ball, causing it to pop up quickly. It's not a difficult shot, but many golfers get ahead of themselves and jerk back the club too quickly.

Here's a way to avoid the jerks: Cock the wrists before you swing.

A strange way to address the ball, perhaps—but it works. Take your normal stance at address; then *without* moving your hands, move the clubhead to a point about six inches behind the ball and a few inches off the ground. As you move the clubhead, your wrists will cock naturally. You're now in a position to execute the backswing and pull off the shot perfectly.

123 Dancing on the Dance Floor

It's tough to make a wedge shot curve to the right or to the left (at least it's tough to do so *deliberately*). So you're limited in what you can conjure up with this club.

In a sense. But this doesn't mean you can't influence the movement of the ball with a wedge. When your ball hits the green, it will be spinning; and if you hit the shot correctly, you can make the ball *bounce* to the left or to the right.

Let's say you want your ball to land to the left of the flag and bounce to the right (perhaps the flag is set behind a bunker that presents a difficult carry). Approach this shot as you would a cut shot: Open your stance slightly, open the clubface, aim a little to the left, and then swing from outside to in, across the ball.

To make your ball land and then bounce to the left, do the opposite: Close your stance, close the clubface, aim a little to the right, and swing from inside to out.

The key to remember is this: With wedge shots, what you lose in the air you can make up for on the ground.

124 Through the Bag

A key to good chipping is to get the ball rolling on the green as soon as possible. And as you're likely to face chips of varying length during a round, it's a good idea to practice your chipping with as many different clubs as possible. Rarely, though, do you see golfers doing this. In fact, many golfers don't practice chipping at all.

All you need is a practice green that isn't too crowded. Drop a bunch of balls by the green (just let them fall, so you end up with different lies). Now hit different shots to different holes, beginning with the sand wedge and working your way through to the 5-iron.

You won't have the luxury of hitting to different holes once you're out on the course. Here, then, is a good rule of thumb for club selection: Take the club with the least amount of loft needed to get the ball to the edge of the putting surface on its first bounce.

125 When Not to Roll

About the only times you should aim to fly a ball high to the pin are:

- when you do not have much green to work with (you might also have a hazard or two between you and the hole)
- when the grass is wet and therefore not conducive to rolling
- when the grass is patchy and your ball might be "thrown" off-line
- when you're hitting from sand

126 Top It

Why, you might well ask, would anyone want to top the ball?

Because more than anything a golfer wants to make solid contact, and hitting the top half of the ball ensures that.

Your next question: Shouldn't you make solid contact by hitting under the ball? Ideally, yes. But golfers become so wrapped up in getting the club to the correct impact point that they *forget* to make solid contact and end up hitting a poor shot.

In addition, golfers tend to think of the chip shot as a full shot hit with half the heft, so they lay off actually hitting the ball and hit behind it (this is called chili-dipping).

By keeping your hands ahead of the ball and hitting down onto the top three-quarters, you will guarantee good contact and move the ball up and out of its lie.

127 A Bigger Hole

A good way to lag the ball close when putting is to try to leave it inside an imaginary three-foot-wide circle around the hole. You can do likewise when chipping, only this time you should imagine that the hole is larger, about four feet wide.

One of the more vivid images is that of a large flowerpot; the flagstick is a flower planted in the middle of the pot.

This imagery works well for two reasons:

1. When you don't feel you have to hole the chip—or even leave it on the lip of the hole—you'll be under less pressure and likely will strike the ball better.

2. If you do hit the ball into the "flowerpot," you'll be close enough to tap in easily.

128 The Line Drive

The worst thing you can do when chipping is to allow the wrists to break as you make contact with the ball.

It is possible to keep the wrists firm just by concentrating on doing so, but we recommend that you try this simple drill: Adopt your normal stance at address and imagine that a line extends from your left shoulder directly down to the clubface.

If you concentrate on keeping your left hand exactly on that line during the chip, your wrists should stay firm and you should make consistently good contact.

129 The Reverse Overlap

Many top pros use their putting grips when chipping, the reason being that it helps them keep their wrists firm. But firm wrists can mean less feel, and those who are said to have great "touch" around the green are the golfers with great feel.

So here's a chipping grip that gives you firmness *and* feel: the reverse overlap.

The conventional overlap grip has the pinkie of the right hand overlapping the index and middle fingers of the left hand. With the reverse overlap, the index finger of the left hand overlaps the ring and little fingers of the right hand.

With more of the fingers of your right hand on the grip, your feel will be better, because while the left hand is usually the "control" hand, the right hand is where you derive your "feel." And because you're still using what is fundamentally a putting grip, your grip will be firm.

The best of both worlds, in other words.

130 Swing Harder to Land Softer

At a tournament in Florida many moons ago, I stood by the practice green and watched a young pro by the name of Pat McGowan impart short-game wisdom on another pro by the name of Mike Reid. Although both were speaking very softly to each other, I came to understand the lesson. McGowan was demonstrating to Reid that the harder you hit a short chip, the shorter the distance it will travel.

This took some swallowing, but I put McGowan's lesson into action when I returned north, and it worked immediately. The principle is this: If you use a very lofted club and accelerate the clubhead just before impact, you impart more backspin on the ball and you take away its roll.

Start by going through all the normal chipping procedures—ball played off right foot, hands ahead of the ball—but as you come within a foot or so of the ball, accelerate *slightly.* Even the slightest acceleration will work.

Open the clubface even more than you think necessary, as this will give you even more loft, and also will compensate should you accidentally close the clubface as you make your slight acceleration.

131 Mark It

You would never think twice about asking another golfer to mark his ball when it is sitting on your putting line. So why would you hesitate to do so when his ball is on your chipping line?

It always makes perfect sense to clear the way when your ball must spend any time on the ground—and further, there is no rule against having a player mark his ball when it's not on the green.

I remember watching Tom Kite and Peter Jacobsen play the second hole at Royal St. George's Golf Club in England during the 1983 British Open. Kite's ball was ten to fifteen yards short of the green. Jacobsen's was about sixty yards short. When he asked Kite to mark his ball, I thought he was kidding. There was no way he could hit it.

Well, Kite marked his ball and Jacobsen's bounce-and-run bounced within inches of the mark. Jacobsen was simply playing the percentages—and playing them correctly.

132 Pin In?

You bet. There is no good reason for removing the flagstick from the hole for shots around the green—especially when you don't have to.

According to the rules, you are penalized two strokes for hitting the flagstick with a putt. So if there's no penalty, why take it out?

The common answer is that the ball might hit the flagstick and bounce out. But this doesn't make sense because:

- A ball that hits the flagstick and bounces out again likely was hit so hard that hitting the flagstick was a benefit rather than a curse. Had the ball *not* hit the flagstick, it might have gone way past the hole.

- Players worry that the ball might hit a flagstick that is leaning against the side of the hole. But that's a reason not for removing the flagstick but rather for making sure it's standing in the hole properly before you hit your shot.

Numbers back this up. In the December 1990 issue of *GOLF Magazine,* Dave Pelz, a short-game teacher and analyst, reported that when he used a special putting device, 33 percent more putts from off the green fell with the pin in than with it out. For a real golfer the result was 18 percent. How thorough was Pelz's testing? This thorough: Man and machine hit a total of ten thousand putts.

If you're concerned that these data reflect *putts* and not chips, don't be. Once a ball is rolling on a green, what club hit it is irrelevant.

133 The Top-Tier Shot

When you are chipping to a flagstick that is cut on the top level of a two-tier green, and you lie just off the lower level of the green, on no account should you think of carrying the ball all the way to the hole. You'll have a far better chance of getting close if you get your ball rolling.

Your lie probably is not that good—you're either in short rough or on fairway grass that is too short to get a club under and still hit a soft lob shot. So your chances of reaching and holding the second tier are slim.

If you get your ball rolling, however, the worst that will happen—barring a complete flub—is that you'll hit past the hole. But at least your putt won't have to climb the slope too.

134 Blade It

If you've ever watched the top players using a wedge from around the green, you've probably seen some of them blade the ball. This is deliberate. It's a shot they go to when their lie is so thick that they cannot hit firmly enough to combat the rough and still hit the ball delicately.

If you think that a putter would be a better choice of club, bear in mind that your putter won't be able to cut through the thick grass and meet the ball squarely.

This is where the wedge comes in. Its lofted face will cut through the grass, and you can use its leading edge as, effectively, the face of your putter.

Address the ball as you would a putt, then strike it sharply on its equator.

The ball likely will come out with some topspin, and initially you'll find yourself hitting past the hole. Practice will make perfect.

135 Open to Square

Although you should open your stance on chips and other short shots, you should not open your shoulders.

Opening your shoulders—having them point left of the target line—will force you to swing across your body, from outside to in, and you will likely cut across the ball and make less-than-solid contact.

The correct procedure is to keep the shoulders square and the hands ahead of the ball throughout the chip.

136 The Bounce-and-Run

The bounce-and-run is useful where you don't have any hazards in front of the green, where the ground in front of the green is firm (as opposed to lush and well watered), or where the ground slopes down toward the green. (It's also a great shot to take on vacation, should you be going to play the firm seaside courses of Scotland and Ireland.)

Play this shot from about sixty yards

from the green, or closer. Use an iron, but no lower than a 5-iron. Open your stance slightly and play the ball almost off your right foot. By keeping your hands ahead of the ball, you'll automatically deloft, or "hood," the club (which is why a lofted iron still works for this low shot).

The complicated part of the shot, however, is not the execution but the calculation, and you may have to practice this one before perfecting it. It's kind of like reading a putt. You must work out where you want your ball to end up, and then work *backwards* to the ball, considering all the bumps and slopes between you and your target area.

Keep most of your weight on your left foot, swing the club back halfway, and then punch down and through the ball. As long as you don't break your wrists or swing too hard, your ball will start bouncing and running toward its target.

137 The Weak Chip

To keep your left wrists from collapsing on chips, weaken the grip of your left hand.

This doesn't mean you should grip less tightly. Weakening the grip means that you should move your left hand to the left, in a counterclockwise direction. If your wrists had broken, your left hand would have moved to the position it now occupies, so you've effectively taken the break out of your wrists.

Notice also that the back of your left hand now faces down your target line. Keep the hand moving toward the target when you chip, and you'll be right on line.

138 The Marble Method

To keep your clubface at the correct angle when you chip, imagine that you're balancing a marble on the face as you swing.

The only way you can prevent the marble from falling off is to swing slowly and to keep the face at exactly the same angle. If you twist it in any direction, the marble will roll off. And if you swing too hard, you will swing out from underneath the marble. By the same token, the marble will roll off if you make a jerky motion when beginning your downswing.

139 The Toe-Poke

If your ball is sitting in the thick stuff beside the green, and you can't get the clubhead on the ball without swinging harder than you'd like, you may want to consider hitting the ball with the *toe* of your putter.

Turn your putter so that the face is perpendicular to the direction you want to hit. When you swing, the thin clubhead will cut through the grass a lot easier than the leading edge of a wedge would. Just remember to give your ball no more than a short, sharp jab, and be careful not to swing too far back.

Another thing to remember: The toe of a putter doesn't have a very big hitting area, so do everything you can to ensure solid contact.

EIGHT

Putting

140 Ready, Aim—Fire!

One of the worst things a golfer can do is think too much about putting. It's better to take one quick look at the line from behind the ball and another from beyond the hole and then hit the putt based on your *first* conclusion.

Too many golfers examine putts from all directions, plumb-bob with their putters—that's the strange exercise that involves dangling the club vertically in front of your face and closing one eye—when they know neither what they're doing nor why they're doing it. Then they stand over the putt, staring at the line until they start seeing all manner of bumps and swales and breaks, and before they know it they're all but frozen stiff and incapable of putting a good roll on the ball.

Trust your instincts, instead—and the first impression usually is based on instinct. Addressing your ball and hitting it swiftly won't necessarily make you hole more putts, but you'll eliminate any opportunity for doubt to creep in and you'll also get into a good rhythm.

Take Two and Run

You won't score well by trying to hole every putt you face. But you will score well by not three-putting.

So unless a putt is within ten to fifteen feet of the hole and has little or no break, you should focus on getting down in two.

A good way to do this is to imagine the hole is three feet in diameter. If you can leave your first putt in the imaginary hole, you should be able to tap your second putt in the real hole because the putt will measure no more than eighteen inches (sixteen inches, actually, as the width of the hole is four inches and change).

Even Ben Crenshaw, considered by many to be the best putter in the game, adopts this approach. He concentrates on the speed of the putt and the tempo of his motion, and thinks only of getting close. He considers every two-putt a success, tries not to get too worked up about misses, and looks on long one-putts as a bonus.

So should you.

142 Strike 'Em Straight

It has been said that every putt is a straight putt, and that holds true even for those putts with double and triple breaks.

That's because no matter where the putt is supposed to end up, it always begins with the blade of the putter striking the ball at an angle perpendicular to the line that the putt must *start out on.* Or look at it this way: Even if a putt breaks sharply downhill and to the right, it still is a straight putt *until it begins to break.*

This isn't a discussion of Zen putting. It's a simple and effective lesson. Golfers have a terrific tendency to "sneak" putts to the hole, but it makes much more sense to decide on the line and then hit the ball straight along it. Let the slope take care of the break.

143 Uphill Blasts

When faced with an uphill putt, don't be afraid to hit it more firmly than you might think necessary.

For one thing, gravity is on your side. Another plus is that the far side of the hole is higher than the near side, so in effect the back of the hole becomes a backstop. Assuming you've chosen the correct line—uphill putts tend not to break much at all—you can then make a run at it safe in the knowledge that when your ball passes over the hole it will fall slightly and hit the "wall" behind the hole—the back of the cup.

144 Don't Be Vague—Putt Like The Haig

Walter Hagen was one of the coolest players in the history of the game. It was said that Hagen's easygoing personality combined with a Gargantuan measure of gamesmanship did the trick.

The truth is, however, that Hagen felt as much pressure as anyone. He just learned how to cope with it. Here's how he did it on the green:

Whenever Hagen found himself jerking at his ball—a sure sign of pressure—he would grip a golf ball with the ring and pinkie fingers of his left hand as he held his putter. The theory was that these fingers were gripping the club too tightly and were causing the jerkiness. After a few swings with the ball in place, Hagen's putting grip usually was loose enough for him to start putting without the ball again.

145 Left Shoulder Low

A common fault among poor putters is the accidental lifting of the head. We say "accidental" because even though the player concentrates on keeping his head still throughout a putt, he has a tendency to lift his left shoulder on the follow-through—and *that* makes the head move up.

You can overcome this fault simply by concentrating on keeping the left shoulder low throughout the putting motion.

When you contact the ball and follow through, keep your left shoulder low. An added benefit: The face of your putter remains square to the target line slightly longer.

146 Disregard Direction

Have you ever noticed how even a high-handicapper will be shocked when a longish putt rolls drastically off-line? That's because *relatively few bad putts miss their target by a considerable margin to the right or left.*

It's true that a putt that reaches the hole has to miss to the right or left, but the really bad misses are putts that are far too long because they've been hit far too hard, or putts that are far too short because they haven't been hit hard enough. How often do you see a putt hit pin-high but ten feet wide of the hole?

The ideal lag putt, therefore, should be struck without any real regard for direction. Length and speed are much more important (and the golfer who thinks about length and speed will get a feel for direction in the process).

If length and speed have been judged correctly, the ball will likely end up in tap-in range—and who knows, a few more long putts might drop in.

147 The Perfect Putting Grip

More and more professionals use what is called the reverse overlap grip when putting.

With the conventional overlap grip, the little finger of the right hand overlaps the left hand, resting in the crease between the index and middle fingers of the left hand. With the reverse overlap, however, the index finger of the left hand overlaps the right hand, resting in the crease between the ring and little fingers.

The reverse overlap helps anchor the hands as a single unit, and that, in turn, helps the hands, arms, and shoulders move as a single unit—a key to good putting.

148 Score on the Rebound

How often have you seen a golfer roll a putt close, watch it creep just past the hole, and then close his eyes and exhale in exasperation as the ball rolls on past the hole?

That golfer just missed a free lesson on how to hit his comeback putt.

If he had watched the line the ball had rolled on once it passed the hole, it would have been simple for him to adjust to the line he needed to hole the comebacker.

The top players know this. They get mad not only when another player steps on their line, but also when he steps on the area immediately behind the hole. They know that the worst a good, aggressive putt is going to leave is an easy comebacker, and they object to others chewing up the turf and making it the slightest bit difficult.

149 The Pro Side

One of the fundamentals of putting across a slope is to make sure that your ball approaches your hole from the high side, otherwise known as the pro side.

First, a ball rolled along the low side would have to defeat the laws of gravity by turning and rolling uphill to reach the hole.

Second, a ball approaching from the high side could do one of three things:

1. roll in the side of the hole nearest to the ball

2. fall in from above the hole, with gravity working properly this time

3. catch the back of the hole and curl in

In other words, a ball hit via the pro side has a pretty good chance of being holed, while a ball hit via the low side has little or no chance at all.

150 Wee Spots of Bother

When putting on wet greens, bear in mind that although you don't have to putt through puddles—those come under "casual water," and you're entitled to putt from the nearest point of relief—you may have to putt over a surface that has patches of extreme dampness.

So you should always check the line

of your putt for the dampest spots, because your putt will slow down when it reaches them. And if you do find unusually damp areas, then be aggressive with your putt.

In fact, you should always putt aggressively on wet greens. Your ball isn't going to roll as fast, and neither is the putting surface going to break as much as it would when dry.

151 Stripes

A ball bearing a red stripe is associated with a practice driving range. But range balls can help you on the putting green.

You can check to see if you're striking the ball squarely by watching what the stripe does once the ball starts rolling.

Find a flat area on your practice green. Address the ball with the stripe aligned down the target line. Hit a putt. Does the line wobble back and forth? If it does, you're coming across the ball at impact and your ball isn't being rolled properly.

Work on your stroke until the stripe appears not to move, and you will improve your putting considerably.

152 Tap Dancing

Watch Gary Player putt. Notice how he crouches low over the ball, anchors his weight by putting most of it on his left side, then makes a very short backswing and "taps" his putter sharply against the back of the ball with very little follow-through.

What he's doing is imparting slight backspin on the ball to stop his putts getting away from him on fast greens.

The principle of this shot can be found in other sports. A Ping-Pong shot hit with backspin requires a sharp slap. To spin a cue ball back, the pool player taps the cue into the back of the ball with no follow-through.

Remember, however, that this is a system for fast greens. If you try it on slower greens, you may find that everything comes up short.

153 Twin Killing

Because the effect of the grain increases as your ball slows down, you should think of long putts with break as *two* putts.

The "first" putt is nothing more than a setup for the "second" putt, and will not break much, as it will be rolling faster. The "second" putt begins when the ball is slowing down and the grain causes the ball to break more.

A good way to figure out long, breaking putts is to work backwards from the hole. Figure out where the ball will have to approach from to get close to the hole, and then hit the "first" putt toward that area.

154 Double Trouble

The relationship between break and speed has a drastic effect on putts that break twice.

If, for instance, you have a putt that appears to break three feet to the right and then three feet to the left, it's not a straight putt. The two do not cancel each other out.

You should actually aim a little to the right because your ball will be rolling slower when it comes to the break to the left, and therefore will be more influenced by the break.

The key, however, is to remember that on putts with more than one break, you should pay more attention to the later breaks than the earlier ones.

155 Slow Train Comin'

A good way to putt on slow or bumpy greens is to change your ball position at address.

Move the ball slightly farther than normal toward your left toe. This will help you hit the ball on the upswing and get it up and rolling over the longer blades of grass or the bumps.

Two caveats when you putt like this:

1. Be careful not to scuff the grass behind your ball.

2. Be mindful of a tendency to pull putts when the ball is farther forward in the stance. Simply concentrate on keeping your wrists firm throughout the stroke.

156 Pick Your Spot

Which would you rather face: a forty-five-foot-long putt or a five-foot-long putt?

Of course you'd prefer the five-footer—but why not turn the long putt into the shorter version?

Once you've settled on the line and speed of a long putt, pick a spot about four to five feet in front of your ball—

on the same line—and concentrate on rolling your ball over that spot.

A case in point: On the seventy-second hole of the 1984 U.S. Open Championship at Winged Foot Golf Club, just north of New York City, Greg Norman was lying three on the fringe of the green and needed to hole a left-to-right downhill curler of some sixteen feet to get into a playoff for the title. He picked out a small brown blemish on the green about eighteen inches in front of his ball and rolled the putt over it ever so gently. The putt dropped, Norman got into the playoff—and was soundly drubbed by Fuzzy Zoeller.

Can't win 'em all!

157 The Perfect Putt

It has been said that the perfect putt is one that would come to a halt seventeen to eighteen inches beyond the cup (if the cup did not exist). The reasoning is that a ball should be rolling firmly when it drops, and "firmly" means that it was hit strongly enough to roll seventeen inches longer than necessary.

So except on drastic downhill putts, you should always count on hitting your putts slightly longer than necessary.

158 Uphill, Downhill

It's frustrating to leave an uphill putt short—as they say, "Never up, never in"—and to smack a downhill putt long. Here's how to avoid both situations:

On uphill putts, aim for an imaginary hole beyond the real hole. You'll be sure of giving the ball enough gas to make it up the hill. On downhill putts, aim for an imaginary hole just *short* of the real hole. Now your ball will be hit delicately enough to crawl down the hole and die in the cup.

159 The Eyes Have It

When you're putting, the best place for your eyes is directly over the ball. Here's why:

If your eyes are inside the line, you'll get a different view of the putt, and you'll aim the putt *relative* to what you see. You'll probably push the ball to the right.

The same goes if your eyes are outside the line, only this time you'll probably pull the putt.

If your eyes are over the ball, however, you can aim the putter exactly as you see the putt.

To make sure your eyes are over the ball, first take your stance and address the ball, then lift your putter up and place the butt end of the grip against the bridge of your nose. Hold the putter so that it hangs loosely and the shaft points directly at the ball. (Move your head to achieve the proper alignment.)

160 Toe It!

When you're nervous about overhitting a delicate downhill putt, you can help yourself by hitting the putt with the toe of the putter.

Putts hit with different parts of the putter's face usually travel different lengths. The sweet spot hits them farthest because that's where the most weight is concentrated. And as the least amount of weight is at the toe—on most putters, that is—it makes perfect sense to use the toe to take some of the power out of the putt.

161 Faster, Not Slower

The biggest mistake high-handicap golfers make on putts inside twelve to fifteen feet is to *decelerate* the putter just before impact. They fear striking the ball too hard, and this leads to all kinds of problems: scuffing the ground behind the ball; opening or closing the face of the putter; topping the ball; leaving the putt way short.

Such players would lower their scores considerably were they to concentrate on *accelerating* the putter through the ball at impact.

To do this, take a short, smooth backswing and then focus on swinging the putter through and beyond the ball, with the wrists firm.

And don't be afraid of hitting the ball too hard. Apart from the fact that the ball has to reach the hole or it won't fall, you'll soon get used to the new feeling and will be able to make the correct adjustments.

162 How to Find the Sweet Spot

You should hit the vast majority of putts with the sweet spot of your putter. The problem, however, is that many putters either don't indicate where the sweet spot is, or indicate a place on the face of the putter that in fact is *not* the sweet spot.

So here's how to find the sweet spot. You'll need a putter and a pencil.

Grasp your putter with one hand and hold it with the blade dangling down. Tap the face of the putter with the butt end of the pencil.

The putter will twist in your hand when you hit any area other than the sweet spot. When you do make contact with the sweet spot, the club will swing back evenly. All that's needed now is a slight scratch on the putter face.

163 Do Think Twice; It's All Right

One of the worst things you can do when you're not sure about a putt, or are interrupted when about to hit, is to go ahead and hit it anyway.

If you notice a break that wasn't there before, or a ball mark that should be repaired; if a fly lands on your ball, or a sudden noise interrupts your train of thought—if any of these things happen, *step away, reread the putt, and start over again.*

Apologize to your playing companions, as it's the polite thing to do, but remember that by stepping away you're likely to take *less* time because you better your chances of holing the putt. If you miss—as you probably will—you'll have to go through the whole routine again on the next putt.

164 Cut That Slice

It's possible to slice a putt, and golfers who do so usually are hitting with the face of the putter open at impact.

Most likely they're standing too close to the ball. They take the club back, then as they swing forward to stroke the ball, they realize they cannot swing comfortably at a ball positioned so close to their feet. So they adjust by pulling their hands and wrists closer to the body, and in doing so, they force the heel of the putter to lead the swing, opening the blade.

To cure this, take your stance a little farther from the ball. Soon you'll be hitting your putts with a square face again.

165 All Change

There is no perfect putting grip because putting is as much a question of comfort and feel as anything else.

The backhanded grip, for instance, is a sure method of keeping your wrists steady throughout the putting motion. It's simply a more drastic version of the reverse overlap grip, which many of the top players in the world employ.

Some golfers prefer to extend the right index finger down the grip. Despite its pejorative name—the "old man's finger"—this grip braces the right wrist throughout the stroke.

Finally, there is that weird grip invented by Bernhard Langer, the German pro who admittedly has suffered from the yips. Larger extends his right *forearm* down the grip and grasps both grip and forearm with his left hand. Everyone criticizes him, but it seems to work—so what's to criticize?

The moral here? Go with what makes you comfortable—let other golfers worry about their own games.

166 Get Used to Missing

The average player who misses several putts becomes despondent, which leads to frustration, which in turn leads the golfer to try to hole putts he has no business trying to hole—which leads to even more putts and even higher scores.

The average player should take solace in the knowledge that even the top players in the world miss one out of every two puts hit from twelve feet.

A few years ago, short-game guru Dave Pelz took a "robot" called the True Roller to the Bethesda Country Club in suburban Washington, D.C., and on a green untrampled by human traffic he had his True Roller hit one hundred twelve-foot putts. It made fifty-four of them. He then went to a nearby daily-fee course, and there the robot made forty-eight.

Human error and the condition of putting surfaces stack the odds against you. This is a just a fact of golfing life, and nothing to get worked up about.

167 Accounting for the Slope

The easiest way to gauge the speed and distance of a putt that must climb a steep slope to an upper tier of a green is to count the slope twice.

If, say, the putt is thirty feet long, and the slope is two feet high, think of hitting a putt that is *at least* thirty-two feet long, because (a) you usually want to err beyond the hole on this kind of putt (the last thing you want to do is to roll back down the slope from the upper tier); and (b) a properly weighted putt always is struck hard enough to roll a foot or two "past" the hole in the event that it doesn't drop.

168 Head Case

It's funny how the shortest putts can be the most nerve-wracking. Why do you stand over a ten-footer and stroke it easily, but fall apart over a tap-in?

Here's a drill to help you tap in short putts firmly and safely: Think of holing the *putter head.*

As you putt the ball, focus on extending the stroke so that the head of your putter reaches a spot above the hole. By the time your putter arrives above the hole, your ball will be safely in it.

169 Right-Shoe Shuffle

This tip is similar to our lesson on handling short putts, except that it is useful on *all* putts.

To make sure that you swing the putter back and return it to the ball perpendicular to the target line, take your stance with your right foot perpendicular to the line. Then, when you swing the putter, concentrate on keeping the face of your putter parallel with the inside of your right foot.

170 Carry Two Putters

A piece of advice that has been making the rounds for decades is that golfers should carry two putters: a heavy putter for slow greens and a light putter for fast greens.

If for any reason one putter doesn't feel right—the thinking goes—then the other one will.

Not a bad theory, and a harmless one if you're not in the habit of carrying the maximum fourteen clubs. If you have room for another club, why shouldn't it be another putter?

171 Aim at the Hole

When you're facing a straight putt or one with just the slightest break, aim at the dead center of the hole.

Sound obvious? Perhaps, but golfers have a strange knack for seeing break that doesn't exist. They look at straight putts and think, "Inside right edge," or "Left lip."

What they should really be doing is aiming at a spot one-quarter of an inch wide, in the dead center of the hole. Now if their putt does move to the right, it has two inches of hole to work with. Ditto to the left.

172 Your Big Break

Golfers trust no one—not even themselves. When facing a putt with a huge break, often they just don't accept that a putt can possibly break that much.

The problem is negative mind-set: Golfers are scared to play so much break. The remedy: Practice putts with a lot of break and *force* the full break.

Go to your practice green and find a putt that breaks significantly. Drop a few balls and then put an obstacle between you and the hole. You can use a golf club or if you're on a quiet practice green, one of the little flagsticks. You can even drop a golf ball or two.

The idea, however, is to get used to hitting putts that need a lot more break than you're comfortable with.

173 A Quick Grain Guide

Greens on most golf courses are either bent grass or Bermuda grass. You can save yourself several strokes—particularly when changing from one grass to another—by learning the difference between the two.

Bent grass is a smoother grass than Bermuda. It is less resistant to heat and therefore is rare in the South (as well as in such vacation areas as Hawaii, the Caribbean, and the Mediterranean). It breaks more than Bermuda grass, and its grain is distinctive: If the grass in front of you has a sheen on it, then it is growing—and the grain is running—away from you. Your putt will be faster. If there is no sheen, then the opposite is true. You can use the same method of reading the sheen if your putt must cross the grain. If the grain is growing downhill, then your putt will break even more, for instance.

Bermuda grass is a wirier grass and has no specific direction to its grain. Think of Bermuda grass as being frizzy hair and bent grass as being straight. Putts on Bermuda, therefore, are liable to roll off-line; the grass almost "throws" them off. So you should hit putts more firmly when playing on Bermuda grass.

Some golf courses seed their greens with hybrids of these two grasses, and in the really cold climates the prevalent grass is what's known as fescue. There also are two wiry types of grass known as Kikuyu and Zoysia, but they're rarer. Just bone up on bent grass and Bermuda and you'll be well prepared for most greens.

174 Outside Influences

We've gone over the two basic types of putting green surfaces: bent grass and Bermuda grass. Now here's a quick rundown of some external factors that affect grain:

- *Water.* Grass grows *toward* water. So if you're playing a lakeside or oceanside course—or even if you're on a green next to a water hazard—figure that the grain will be running toward the water, and read more break into your putts.

- *The Sun.* Grass also likes heat and tends to grow toward the setting sun. So it's not a bad idea to establish which direction is west and figure in more break for that too.

- *Mountains.* Grass tends to grow *away* from mountains, probably because water gathers in lower areas.

175 The Four-Inch Rule

You should aim a putt outside the hole *only when you are sure that there is more than four inches of break.*

Why four inches? Because that's how wide the hole is. Let's say, for example, that you think a putt will break four inches to the left. If you aim at the right lip, you are giving yourself four inches of leeway. If it in fact breaks at one inch, it still will fall in. Ditto two, three, and four inches.

Now let's say that you aim outside the hole by, say, two inches, figuring that the four-inch break will drop your ball in the middle of the hole. If it does break at four inches, it'll do just that. But one inch will miss. So might two inches.

The point is that too many golfers read too much break into their putts. The four-inch rule is designed to make you putt as close to the hole as often as possible.

176 Slow Times

Although golf course superintendents try to keep the speed of their putting surfaces consistent throughout the day, and from day to day, the elements and club schedules thwart even their best efforts. There will be occasions when greens will be slower than usual:

1. Late in the day: Greens are cut at first light and grow throughout the day. So it stands to reason that they'll be longer late in the afternoon. (They'll also be rougher, because of the foot traffic they receive during the day.)

2. On Tuesdays: This applies only at clubs that close on Mondays, the traditional rest day for a golf course. It is nigh impossible for even today's most sophisticated mowers to cut a two-day growth smoothly. For the same reason, your greens will be at their best on Sundays, after several daily mowings.

It's worth noting, too, that the lie of the land also conspires to frustrate a superintendent's efforts toward consistency. A green shaded by trees gets less sunlight than a green in an open area and therefore is not so lush. It likely will be faster than other greens. The same goes for a green in a low-lying area where it does not get the same air circulation as, say, an elevated green.

177 Ship Ahoy!

One of the clearest images of how the hands should operate when putting comes from one George Low, a distinguished player and teacher who specialized in putting.

Low compared the hands to parts of a ship. The left hand, he said, represents the sail of the ship. It provides the "power" and the strength of the putt. The right hand is the rudder. It steers the putt and keeps it under control on a true course.

Think of this image and your hands will soon begin to work in harmony.

178 A Close Move

When you face a short but important putt, you can make it even shorter by playing the ball further back in your stance.

When you move your ball back, your left foot effectively moves even closer to the hole, and that makes the putt feel shorter. Holing these knee-knockers is all about confidence, and the shorter the putt appears, the more confident you will be.

Just make sure you don't hit your foot. That carries a two-stroke penalty.

179 Read the Lip

If, when you putt, you are in doubt about the grain—the direction in which the grass grows—check a very good indicator you'll find on every green: the hole.

Take a look at the rim of the hole

and you'll notice that one side is lined by grass and the other by a sliver of dirt. This means the grain runs *from* the side where the grass is and *toward* the side where the dirt is. Grass lies flat. The reason the dirt exists is that the *hole* is where grass roots would have been. No roots means no grass within the length of a blade. Presto! Dirt.

So you know that the grain runs *toward* the dirt patch.

180 The Stiff-Wrist Drill

Golf inventors have come up with all kinds of contraptions for keeping the left wrists stiff during putts and chips. You don't have to go to such lengths. Go to a sporting goods store and get a wristband (your best bet is the tennis department).

Before practicing, don the wristband, choke down on your putter (or short iron) and simply insert the grip inside the wristband, inside your wrist.

Not only does this teach you how to make your forearm and the putter work as a unit, but also it tells you when your wrist is breaking. When this happens, the putter grip will stretch the inside of the wristband.

181 Heel It

You can help keep your putter face square to the target line by making sure that the heel of the putter passes the ball just as you are about to hit it. Obviously, the heel *should* do so, but the idea is to focus on the heel and not on the striking of the ball.

This doesn't guarantee that the putter comes in squarely so much as it helps you keep your grip firm until after you've struck the ball. A lot of putts are missed when the left side of the grip breaks down and the face of the putter closes. When a golfer says disgustedly, "Ah, pulled it," he's describing exactly what has happened.

Had he kept the heel moving parallel to the target line, he probably wouldn't have missed.

182 Look Three Times

Read the line of your putt from three different positions behind the ball—except when you risk holding up play. Start by reading from directly behind the ball. This will give you your closest look at the whole line, but you'll see less break than there really is (that's why a lot of pros look from the edge of the green). You'll get a better read from about six feet behind your ball, and you can confirm *that* read by moving back another six feet for a third reading.

You also should read putts from the far side of the hole and from the sides. This is a lot of reading, so do it when the course is quiet and when other players are preparing to hit their putts—or don't do it all.

183 When to Grip More Firmly

The only time you should not use a light grip on the golf club is when you face a short putt.

Consistency of grip pressure is key here. When you grip lightly on a short putt, you run the risk of gripping a little bit tighter as you take the club away. This could cause you to open or close the club face.

While it's true that you're likely to grip the club tighter on the takeaway for *every* putt, the margin for error is slimmer on short ones. So grip a little firmer and strike the ball with authority. Short putts, after all, tend not to be touch putts.

184 On the Deck

A good drill for keeping your putter moving along the target line is to keep your putter so low throughout the stroke that at the end of the swing the putter is still touching the ground.

This drill also keeps your wrists firm—if the putter head rises after impact, the wrists most likely have broken.

185 The Name Game

The wording on a golf ball can help your alignment when putting and driving, the two occasions (apart from certain rules situations) when you can place your ball exactly as you want it. To many players that means with the name of the ball pointing down the target line or perpendicular to the line and therefore parallel with the club face.

In an experiment conducted several years ago golf pros were asked whether they always placed the ball with the name of the ball—not the logo—in the same position. All replied that they did.

They then were asked to indicate on a drawing of a ball where they placed it. Slightly more than half positioned the ball so that the name pointed down the target line. Their reasoning was that this gave them a better idea of the angle at which they wanted to swing at impact. For putting, it helped them start the ball on the chosen line.

Those who positioned the ball perpendicular to the target line focused on making the whole club face hit the whole name at the same time, and that helped them contact the ball squarely when putting *and* driving.

186 Longer, Longer

To practice putting with an accelerating stroke, find yourself a long putt on a practice green and then hit it with a disproportionately short backswing.

The only way you will get the ball to the hole will be to exaggerate the downswing and follow-through.

This isn't how you should putt when you get to the golf course, but it will give you a feel for a sound putting stroke: short backswing, accelerated follow-through.

187 The No-Look Stroke

No, we're not referring here to the no-look-at-the-ball-while-you-strike-your-putt fad that was very much in vogue in the mid-1980s. We mean do look at the ball as you strike it, but don't look at the ball again until it's safely in the hole.

This is a good exercise for short putts. On longer putts you will want to read how the putt reacts around the hole, particularly if you hit long and want to get a jump on how your comebacker will roll.

But on short putts when there's little or no break—and certainly none that you should play—the key is to keep your head steady. So do just that—keep it steady until you hear your ball hit the bottom of the cup.

188 Nail It

You'll hit your putts a lot more firmly if you think of your putter as a hammer and imagine that there's a nail in the back of the ball.

We're not advocating that you hit every putt hard, however. When you hammer in a nail, you start with a few gentle taps and progress to harder blows. What's consistent from blow to blow, from tap to tap, is that each strike is *deliberate.* The same goes with putting.

We don't suggest that you apply this lesson to all shots. As you tend to hit iron and wood shots with almost maximum force, the nail analogy may cause you to swing too hard. And that usually leads to loss of balance and poor contact between club and ball.

NINE

Sand Play

189 The General Sand Shot

In general, a sand shot should be hit with a sand wedge, with both the stance and the club face opened wide. The idea is to hit the sand and let it carry the ball out of the bunker. You should aim to make contact with the sand about two inches behind the ball and hit under and through. An important point here: With few exceptions, you should make a full follow-through.

190 The Texas Wedge

There are occasions when it's a good idea to putt out of a bunker—or use the "Texas Wedge." The bunker should have firm sand and little or no lip, and there should be a smooth surface between the ball and the edge of the bunker.

Address the ball as you would a putt, with the ball in the center of your stance. Swing with the arms and shoulders, but keep the wrists firm and the rest of your body, especially your head, absolutely still. The key is to make solid contact.

Be careful not to ground the putter. If you do, you'll be penalized.

191 A Real Money Shot

Visual imagery is common in bunker play. Some instructors tell students to imagine that the face of the club is the palm of their hands, which they "slap" under the ball in the hitting zone. We prefer to think of money.

A dollar bill is slightly more than six inches long. That means that if a bill is laid under a ball, about two inches of the bill would protrude back from the ball. As the ideal explosion shot demands that you hit into the sand roughly two inches behind the ball, you should pretend you're hitting the dollar bill out of the bunker.

This is an especially useful image because in order to hit the bill right out of the bunker, you'll need to complete your follow-through, and that's another important element of just about every sand shot.

192 Down and Out

The sand shot hit from a downhill lie is one of the toughest of all. Here's how to hit it:

The key is ball position. As with other downhill shots, you should play the ball back in your stance, in this case roughly opposite your right foot.

Next, swing the club up abruptly, breaking the wrists. Keeping your legs and torso steady, hit into the sand two inches behind the ball. Follow through normally.

There is not much margin for error on this shot, so once you've picked the spot where you want the club to make contact with the sand, concentrate on hitting that spot and following through.

193 Playing with Abandon

When sand is wet or really firm, your sand wedge with its wide flange may very easily bounce off the surface and blade the ball.

In such circumstances, it's better to use a pitching wedge or, when the flag is a long way off and you want your ball to run more, a 7-, 8-, or 9-iron.

Play your ball back in an open stance (much as you would do when playing a chip from the fairway) and position your hands just ahead of the ball. Unlike most sand shots, this one requires that you concentrate on hitting the ball first, not the sand.

Work out your "landing area" before hitting the shot, and try to hit that area. If you miss it, don't worry. With all sand shots, it's far more important to get out of the sand than to leave your ball close to the hole.

194 Buried Alive?

Hitting from a buried lie in a bunker (otherwise known as a fried egg) isn't as difficult as most golfers think. In fact, the shot that gets the ball out is closer to a "normal" golf shot than a conventional bunker shot is.

That's because you play the shot with your clubface closed. Remember that the flange of a sand wedge is designed to prevent you from digging into the sand. But with a buried lie, digging in is exactly what you want to do.

Close the face of your wedge and hit down into the sand an inch or two behind your ball. This is one of the few sand shots in which a follow-through isn't just unimportant—it shouldn't exist at all. Some golfers have even been known to let the club go at impact.

Note: This shot can also be played with a pitching wedge, which is almost guaranteed to dig in.

195 Cut the Cord

Here's another piece of visual imagery to help you cut your ball out of sand:

Imagine that a thick piece of cord is dangling vertically, just behind your ball. Now, open your stance to help you swing from outside to in, then use the leading edge of your club to "slice" the cord where it touches the sand.

Soon you'll find yourself opening the blade properly and cutting through the ball the way the pros do.

196 Run It Up

The delicate explosion shot—puff of sand; ball flies to the hole and stops on a dime—is tough to hit consistently. Most attempts see the ball rolling more than expected. So why not anticipate the roll and play for it?

The idea is to take the spin out of the shot by hitting even farther behind the ball than usual—three or four inches is recommended—and compensating for the removal of power by making a full swing.

Your ball will explode out of the sand but will roll a good three or four yards.

197 Super Slo-Mo

Sand shots put such fear in the hearts of most golfers that they rush the shot and swing fast and jerkily, thus making the good sand shot a matter more of happenstance than of planning and skill.

The simple way to remedy this fault is to swing as *slowly* as possible. You'll find this lesson useful all over the golf course, but it is most useful in sand.

Remember that the whole point of the sand shot is to miss the ball. You hit the sand, and the sand lifts the ball out of the bunker. Swinging faster usually doesn't help.

Swinging very slowly will give you a greater feel of hitting the sand behind the ball, take the tension out of the shot, and ultimately give you the confidence to play any shot out of sand.

198 Face Left, Aim Straight

Here's a simple way of remembering how much to open the blade of your sand wedge.

Take an open stance, with your feet aiming to the left of the hole. Then simply open the club face until it is aiming directly *at* the hole.

Now swing outside-to-in across the ball, and your ball will pop out and bounce and roll slightly to the right, toward the hole.

199 No Wrists, No Risk

Excessive wrist action can wreck a golf shot. It usually leads to topping or blading, which in a greenside bunker can be especially ruinous. There's usually not much golf course around greens, and a ball bladed out of a bunker could end up in a water hazard, out of bounds, or in some other unplayable lie.

It's a good idea, therefore, to hit all sand shots with stiff wrists—even those that require you to cock your wrists early on the backswing.

Remember: No wrists, no risk.

200 The Long Bunker Shot, Part One

The long bunker shot is one of the easiest shots to play and one of the most satisfying in the entire game.

Here are the six fundamentals of the bunker shot:

1. Choke down on the grip of the club to compensate for having to dig your feet into the sand to anchor your body.

2. Do not move the legs during the swing.

3. Take two or sometimes three extra clubs to make up for distance lost by the arms-and-hands-only swing. If you're within reach of the green, take as much club as you'll need for the ball to land near the hole. Because you're hitting down into the back of the ball, the ball should have enough spin on it to stop quickly.

4. Play the ball in the middle of your stance so you make contact just before the bottom of your swing arc.

5. Always hit the ball first.

6. Don't ground your club. That's a two-stroke penalty.

201 The Long Bunker Shot, Part Two

One way to prevent dipping and hitting your ball heavy when playing a long bunker shot is to concentrate on keeping the knees on the same level throughout the swing.

Note that we say "on the same level" and not just "level." The idea is to stop you from lifting up or bending down. If you lift up, either you hit the ball thin or you run the risk of hitting it fat if you bend down again. If you bend down first, you'll almost definitely hit the ball fat.

202 On a Roll

A ball hit from wet sand will spin less than one hit from dry, fluffy sand. So aim short of the hole and make a shorter swing than you usually would.

203 Shoulder the Slope

The worst thing about hitting an uphill sand shot is that your ball probably is plugged in the sand. Balls that aren't plugged usually roll back down to a flat area.

Here's how to play the shot: Anchor your body by planting your right foot solidly in the sand, and slant your shoulders so that they are parallel with the slope.

The swing for this shot isn't pretty. Just pick up the club sharply, keeping your legs still, and whack the sand behind the ball. Don't try to follow through. Remember that in such a perilous position *any* recovery is a good recovery.

204 No Unpleasant Bending

One of the most awkward bunker shots calls for you to stand outside the bunker when your ball is inside it. This usually results in unpleasant bending and a loss of balance.

The key here is not to bend the back and stretch down to the ball. Concentrate instead on bending the knees as much as possible.

Think of weight lifters. You never see them bending over to pick up their weights. They bend their knees, grab the weights, then simply stand up. Their legs are doing the lifting.

Your legs, too, should do the bending on these tough bunker shots.

205 Left-Arm Heft

In a sand shot the most important part of the body is the left arm.

Think of your left arm as holding a tennis racket hitting a backhand shot (a good image for most shots, but especially so for sand shots). The left arm initiates the takeaway and controls the downswing and follow-through. It also helps you firm your left side.

If you focus too much on your right arm, your left side is likely to collapse, your wrists may break, and you could very easily end up skulling the ball out of the bunker and into further trouble across the green.

A few years ago Fred Couples secured a victory in a PGA Tour event by holing a greenside bunker shot in which he took his right hand off the club at impact and swung through with his left arm only. He was able to play the shot because he kept the most important part of his body in control of the club.

206 Use Your Feet

Don't take digging and planting your feet for granted.

Digging your feet into sand will give you a firm base with which to hit the shot. Also it will tell you what you're dealing with: how soft or coarse the sand is, how deep it is, whether there's a layer of hardpan just under the surface.

Be careful when digging in, however. If you dig in *too* deeply, and then fill in your footprints, you will be guilty of "building a stance," which is a breach of Rule 13-3. The penalty is two strokes in stroke play or loss of a hole in match play.

207 The Toughest Shot in Golf

Ask any pro the toughest shot in golf and he'll say the sixty-yard sand shot. Even the top players have trouble deciding whether this calls for an explosion shot or a normal wedge shot.

Fortunately, we average players don't have to make that decision. The sixty-yard explosion just isn't in our bags. So we'll make do with the normal wedge shot.

Stand squarely, with the ball in the middle of your stance. As with the long bunker shot, you should make contact with the ball first, so remain as steady as possible for as long as possible. As this requires you to swing with only your hands and arms, you'll want to take a club or two more than usual (but bear in mind that playing the ball farther back than normal will deloft the club face slightly).

For anything up to seventy-five yards, the average player should use a pitching wedge hit with a three-quarters swing.

208 Following in Someone's Footsteps

Landing in someone else's footprint in a bunker can be very frustrating—especially if there are rakes stationed around the sand. But getting worked up about someone else's misdeeds won't help you escape.

The trick here is to treat your ball as though it were in a buried lie. Pick up the club sharply and hit sharply down behind the ball to avoid the surrounding "barrier" of sand. You may also want to adjust your angle of attack depending on how the footprint lies.

The only real difference between the footprint shot and the buried lie shot is that you use a sand wedge and not a pitching wedge. You want to dig through the sides of the footprint—hence the angle of attack—but beyond that it's a normal sand shot.

209 Don't Be Deceived

When your ball is sitting up in sand on a rise that is caused by, say, someone's footprints, don't be fooled into thinking this is an easy shot. Players tend to try to nip the ball off the surface of the sand, or take too much sand in an effort not to hit it too far. Do the former and you may blade the ball. Do the latter and you may hit it fat.

This is an instance where you'll want to hit not under the ball but down and through it. Pick your spot, about two inches behind the ball—and slightly below it, because of the rise—and swing as you would for a normal chip shot. If you're still worried about hitting too far, move your weight back to your right foot. This will force you to swing more with your arms and will take some oomph out of the shot.

210 Bigger Bull's-Eye

Because every golfer wants to get up and down from greenside sand, there is always great pressure to hit the ball close from a bunker.

The fact is, however, that a top pro who gets up and down *half* the time is doing very well indeed.

For this reason you should not concentrate on hitting sand shots to tap-in range—that is, to within three feet—as you would do for a long putt.

Focus instead on hitting to within a target that's, say, twelve to fifteen feet in diameter. That gives you up to seven and a half feet to play with on each side of the hole and a much easier bull's-eye to deal with. You'll be more relaxed and will hit your ball even closer.

211 Tee-Time

Trying to hit a tee from under your ball is a good drill for getting your drives in the air. It's also a good drill for sand play. Here's how it's done:

Tee up your ball in a bunker, and tee it up high. Hit the tee from under the ball. Now tee it so that the tee is just barely showing. Hit it out again.

Now position the ball so that no part of the tee is visible; the bottom of the ball is flush with the sand. Practice until you can consistently hit the tee out of the sand, then play the same shot while *pretending* that the tee is still under the sand.

The lesson here is that the golfer hits the sand and the sand lifts the ball out of the bunker. So at no point should you think of hitting the ball itself.

212 Twice as Far

A good way to gauge distance on a sand shot is to think of hitting the ball twice as far.

Let's say you have a sand shot of

twenty-five feet. Hit it with the same power that you would use for a fairway shot of fifty feet.

A word of warning: This system works well on medium to long sand shots. On the short, "touch" shots you're better off practicing to get a feel for finesse. After all, you may well have a six-foot-long sand shot, but how many twelve-foot-long fairway shots do you ever have?

TEN

Trouble Play

213 Your Top Priority

When you find yourself in rough, forget about pulling off a miraculous recovery and take the quickest and easiest way out.

Go to a wedge or 9-iron and hit to the nearest area of fairway (assuming you have an opening).

If you have a clean lie and can make a good swing at your ball, then you could be a bit more adventurous and go to a middle iron or a lofted wood.

Otherwise, play it safe. Average golfers waste too many strokes by attempting impossible shots that only put them in worse situations.

214 The Impact Keys

Here are two swing keys to think of when you're hitting out of a rough with a middle or a short iron:

1. *Open your club face.* The rough tends to pull the face of a club shut as you swing through it, with the result that, the grass may deloft, say, a 7-iron into a 4- or a 5-iron.

2. *Keep the wrists firm.* Although opening the club face suggests that you expect the grass to close the face, you still should hit with firm wrists. The worst that can happen is that you hit with too much loft and give yourself an even better chance of getting out of trouble.

215 Double Trouble

When you find yourself in greenside rough with more trouble between you and the hole—a bunker, for example—it's not a good idea to try to clear one area of trouble from another.

The first option you have is to take more than enough club to take the second hazard out of play.

The second option is to hit to a safe area, to the right or left of the second hazard. It may be a roundabout way of getting home, but at least you'll arrive there.

216 Ball Above Your Feet

When hitting a ball that lies above your feet on a hill, you should follow these principles:

• Put more of your weight on the toes of your feet. This will improve your balance and keep you from falling backwards as you swing.

• Grip down the shaft. Obviously the ball is closer to your hands than it would be on a flat lie, so you must effectively shorten the shaft.

• Don't make a full swing. This is a control shot, so swing back no farther than the three-quarters position.

• Take more club than you need. You're gripping down and swinging at three-quarters strength, so compensate by taking two extra clubs (a 4-iron instead of a 6-iron, for example).

• Aim to the right of your target. This shot has a tendency to fly to the left.

217 Ball Below Your Feet

These are the principles for hitting a ball that lies below your feet on a hill:

- Put more weight than usual on your heels. This will prevent you from falling forward.

- Don't make a full swing. Balance is key to making solid contact, so you will want to do everything to maintain good balance. Swinging no farther than the three-quarters position helps a lot.

- Take more club than usual. Although you will not be gripping down the shaft, as you should do when the ball is above your feet, you still must compensate for not making a full swing.

- Aim to the left of your target. This shot has a tendency to fly to the right.

218 Uphill Shots

Follow these principles when hitting uphill:

- Take more club than you would need for the same distance on a flat lie. When you address the ball, your clubface will effectively be more lofted and your ball will fly higher.

• Tilt slightly to your right so your lie becomes less hilly. But don't tilt back so far that you run the risk of losing your balance.

• Restrict your shoulder action; swing more with your arms.

219 Downhill Shots

Follow these principles when hitting downhill:

• Take one or two clubs less than what you would use on a level lie. The hill effectively delofts the clubface. In addition, if the hill continues to slope downward into and through the landing area, your ball will likely roll more after it lands.

• Play the ball farther back in your stance so you don't thin it or blade it.

• Keep the left side of your lower body firm. It's vital that you stay down on the ball. You want to hit through it to prevent thinning it.

• Don't make a full shoulder turn. Swing more with your arms.

220 Handling the Flyer

"Flyer" refers to a lie where grass is likely to get between the clubface and your ball at impact. The grass doesn't allow the grooves of the club to impart backspin on the ball, and the ball flies farther and doesn't stop so fast.

There is not much you can do about the lie. You certainly can't tamp the grass down or remove it—that's against the rules. The only real solution open to you is to compensate by taking less club and aiming short of your target.

If there's trouble in front of your target (a pond, perhaps, or a large bunker), it's best to let the flyer carry your ball past the flagstick. Not such a bad option when one considers that on most golf courses the trouble is in front of the green or at the sides.

Plug Luck

When your ball is plugged, or embedded, it's not important to know how to hit out of such a lie. It is, however, important to be familiar with the Rules of Golf. In most cases, you get a free drop.

According to the rules, a ball that is "embedded in its own pitchmark" may be lifted, cleaned, and dropped as close as possible to where it lay (but no closer to the hole). Note that the rules allow you to clean the ball; if it plugged, it likely did so in muddy ground, so your ball might well have mud clinging to it. Be sure to clean it.

The rules also specify that you get free relief only in "closely mown" areas "through the green." This means anywhere on the course except tees, greens, hazards, and rough (paths cut through rough are considered closely mown areas, however).

The truth is that most golfers play the embedded-ball rule in the rough as well. It's official only when a local rule validates the practice, but no one in your weekend foursome is going to complain if you invoke the local rule when necessary.

222 Water, Water, Everywhere

There are two ways to play water shots. The first, and probably the wiser, option is to take a penalty stroke and drop your ball on dry land (check your rules book for your options).

The second should be used only when your ball is barely under the surface; if it's any deeper, you should resort to Option One.

First, take off your shoes and socks and roll up your pants. Next, address the ball. Make sure that your clubhead does not touch the water—this will save you a two-stroke penalty.

You'll succeed in hitting the ball only if the leading edge of the club enters the water *just behind the ball.* The leading edge "cuts" into the water cleaner than any other part of the clubhead; and you should hit behind the ball because when your club enters the water it still has a short distance to travel before it reaches the bottom of the swing and the base of the ball.

Remember also that water, like long grass or sand, will decelerate your clubhead. So keep your wrists and hands firm and concentrate on swinging through the ball.

The Low Blow

Let's say your ball comes to rest in or around trees. Although you can make a full swing, some branches are sticking out on your target line. The safest play is a low, running shot under the branches. Here's how to hit it:

Take a club with enough loft to get you out of your lie, but not so much that the ball will fly up and hit the branches. Next, visualize the ball coming off the club face and decide how hard you'll want to swing the ball.

Play the ball slightly back in your stance; make your usual backswing, but shorten the follow-through of your downswing and *make sure you finish low.*

Be careful not to jerk at the ball. In fact, it's not a bad idea—so long as you don't hold up play—to practice a few slow, low swings before you hit.

224 More Than Enough

A good rule of thumb for hitting from steep sidehill lies is to take two more clubs than you would need when hitting from a flat lie.

Let's say the ball lies above your feet on a steep slope, 150 yards from the green. One option is to take your normal 150-yard club and aim to the right to compensate for the hooking curve that such lies cause. This is not a good idea, because to hit that distance with that club, you'll have to make a full swing, which will probably knock you off balance.

The reason for taking two more clubs is that it forces you to swing easier and maintain better balance. You should still aim to the right, because your ball will fly right to left from this type of lie, but the key is to keep the shot under control.

225 Sand or Rough?

It's not uncommon to find a sandy lie outside a bunker on seaside courses or courses that are maintained poorly, particularly around bunkers.

The main problem with this type of lie is that it is unpredictable. You can never tell whether it's soft enough to hit an explosion shot, or whether it's too soft to hit a normal recovery shot.

So it's best here to concentrate on making contact and getting the ball moving.

You'll want to hit a sharp punch shot. Position the ball slightly farther back in your stance, and swing the club back to the half or three-quarters position. Break your wrists early on the backswing, then bring the club down into the ball with a firm left wrist. Throughout the swing you should use little leg action; excessive leg action can jeopardize your chances of hitting the ball crisply.

226 In the Deep Stuff

When your ball ends up in deep rough, you may well drop one stroke; but take solace in the fact that a good recovery will likely prevent you from dropping two or more.

So here's how to recover: Take a club with a lot of loft. Break the wrists early in the backswing. Keeping your wrists firm, hit sharply down into the back of the ball, and be sure to *hit the ball first.* This will prevent the grass from snagging the club head and causing you to muff the shot.

Remember, this is a sharp up-and-down swing designed to pop your ball to safety.

227 Delivery from Divots

You may not move a ball that lands in a divot hole. But you can escape. It's a matter of club selection and special execution.

Your ball is for all intents and purposes in a hole, so you should take a club with enough loft to get it out. But don't make the mistake of opening the club face. You want to cut down and through the sides of the divot hole, and opening the blade could cause the bottom of the club to bounce off the ground. In the same vein, don't use a wood for this shot. Its flat sole also will bounce.

Instead, you should "hood" the club face—deloft it—and set up with your stance slightly open. The ball should be played from just inside your right foot, with your hands well ahead of the ball.

Swing back and then swing sharply down into the ball, keeping your hands forward. Your ball will come out fast, and very likely hot, so allow for the roll by taking one less club than you normally would for the distance.

228 Drop down a Gear

When the wind is behind you on a tee shot, resist the temptation to crank up your swing to try to catch the jet stream. Any attempt to overswing will result in a miserable flail at the ball that either hits it badly off-line or hardly makes decent connection at all. You waste the wind, in other words.

It's a better idea to swing easier when the wind is behind you, because the easier you swing, the better your chances of making solid contact.

229 Widen in the Wind

In the normal stance the feet are positioned at approximately shoulder width. This allows an easy hip and body turn. In windy weather, however, such a stance may become unstable, so you should widen your stance slightly.

Not so much that your legs are stretched out, however—just enough to provide a more solid anchor for your swing.

230 Playing Well in the Wind

Whenever you face a shot to a green in a crosswind, remember that a firm, well-struck *straight* shot rarely is affected much by wind.

In most instances, a ball that is blown significantly off-line—say, from right to left—already has been hit on that trajectory. A draw that gets caught by the wind quickly turns into a big hook.

So if you're playing in wind and happen to be hitting the ball solidly, aim and hit your ball directly at your target. Even if the wind does influence your ball, it will not be by much.

231 The Best Foul-Weather Tip of All

It doesn't matter whether it's raining hard, blowing a gale, or pelting down hail the size of, well, golf balls. You are going to drop shots in bad weather.

But you can minimize the amount you drop by working on your short game.

A sharp short game cuts strokes off your score in any conditions, but it's especially valuable when the elements are conspiring to make your score soar.

232 Wet Chips

Judging distance and roll on a wet green is difficult. The wet grass usually will cause your ball to pull up quickly, but there are occasions when your ball will skip quickly when it first lands.

The best strategy is to eliminate the guesswork. Take a wedge (a sand wedge, or a pitching wedge for tight lies) and hit a soft, high lob as close to the hole as possible. The shape of the shot will stop your ball from skipping, but the wet grass will still cause it to pull up quickly.

233 And on Wet Greens

Wet greens are slower than dry greens, which means they don't roll so fast and they don't break so much.

Be more aggressive when you putt on a wet green, and go for the hole more often. Allow for less break and give the putt a good run. Even if you put too much power into the putt, the green will be slow enough that you shouldn't have too tough a comebacker. The only caveat is that you should not hit the putt harder by swinging back farther. An overswing can lead to an off-center hit, a hit with an open or closed face—or the sudden fear that you're going to hit too far, which you counter by decelerating the putter. You should hit your putts harder by *accelerating* through the ball.

234 Push It in the Wind

The image of pushing the ball with the right hand crops up frequently in golf. Imagining that your right palm is the face of your putter can help on short putts. Imagining that your right hand is tossing a ball toward the hole can help on chips. But the right-hand image is most useful when you're hitting iron shots into a stiff wind.

You'll want to take two or three clubs more than you usually would for the distance, for two reasons: (1) you want to keep the ball low, and (2) the obvious reason, the wind is blowing in your face.

To hit the shot, grip down the shaft, keep your weight on your left side, and make a full swing. As you approach impact, imagine that your right hand is going to push the ball toward the target. This will cause you to keep the club face square to the target line longer—and in a headwind the last thing you want to do is hook or slice; it will also shorten your follow-through and force you to "punch" the ball. As any good iron player will tell you, a punch shot is a key weapon in dealing with strong winds.

235 Work the Wind

In most cases you'll struggle to play the wind. But if you know how to hit a draw and a fade, you can make the wind work for you when you want to hit a particular target and when you want maximum distance. Here are four situations:

1. The wind is from left to right, and you want to hit a target: Draw the ball from right to left, into the wind.

2. The wind is from left to right, and you want distance: Cut the ball from left to right and ride the wind.

3. The wind is from right to left, and you want to hit a target: Cut the ball from left to right, into the wind.

4. The wind is from right to left, and you want distance: Draw the ball from right to left and ride the wind.

236 Turning Southpaw

There will be occasions when you can advance your ball only by hitting it left-handed (or right-handed if you're a natural leftie).

If you choose to use an iron, make sure it's a wedge. Not because of its loft—by turning the club around you de-loft the face anyway—but because it's got the largest club face and therefore the smallest margin of error.

Also, consider using your putter. If it's a cavity-back model, like many of the Ping models, you might even be able to get your ball up in the air. Just be sure to punch it. If you follow through with one of these putters, you may well end up tossing your ball back over your head!

If you carry a putter whose back and front sides have the same shape, like the Spalding Bulls Eye, then you won't have to turn the putter around to hit.

Another thing to remember is that if you're in the habit of carrying fewer than fourteen clubs, then you could add a left-handed club for those rare occasions when you become a southpaw.

237 Abolish Your Backswing

If your ball comes to rest in an area in which you can't get a full swing on the ball, you may want to hit with only part of your swing.

Let's say your ball comes to rest close to a tree. If you can swing your club back to calf level or, better still, to the height of your knees, and if the lie isn't too difficult, there still is a shot you can play.

Address the ball with a lofted club. Then, very slowly, swing the club back as far as it will go. Now freeze. Your wrists should be cocked.

From here, chop down into the back of the ball. It should pop out—not that far, but away from further trouble.

This shot is especially valuable when your only other option is to drop the ball in an area where a drop will mean even more trouble.

238 Keep Your Eye on the Ball

When you hit a shot off-line and into trouble, the worst thing you can do is to take your eyes off the ball. You might well lose it.

The best thing you can do in this case is to *concentrate on watching* the ball until it lands. Now pick out a particular spot—a branch or rock, perhaps—and focus on it. Keep watching it.

When everyone has hit, start walking toward the spot. Chances are, you'll find your ball. And chances are, you'll save yourself, and your playing partners, time.

The only time you should avert your eyes is when hitting a provisional ball: Hit the provisional, and then go back to the exact spot where you stood to hit the first ball, pick out your target, and proceed toward it.

The key is never to think of a general direction or a general area in which your ball may have come to rest.

239 Cleanup Time

Wet weather always means clogged spikes. Wet grass on a fairway will cling to the soles of your golf shoes, and you can fully expect to emerge from any trouble areas with all manner of dirt and leaves hanging from your shoes.

When playing on wet turf, you should constantly be aware of the condition of your golf shoes and should always check that your spikes are free of any debris before you swing.

Spikes help give you a solid foundation for the swing, so clearly they're even more valuable on wet, slippery ground. But of what use are spikes if your soles are so clogged that the points can't dig into the turf?

240 Hot Stuff

Oppressive heat makes the game very difficult. Your body can overheat and dehydrate; your hands can perspire; the strength can be sapped from your body very easily. For some players it's tougher to score in hot conditions than in wind, cold, and rain.

So here are a few hot-weather tips:

• Wear a hat with a bill. Apart from protecting your scalp, it will stop you from squinting all day.

• Wear a light wristband on your glove hand. Failing that, use a golf glove with a terry-cloth strap (Slazenger makes one, for example).

• Drink liquids before, during, and after your round.

• Don't eat a heavy meal before a round. Snack during a round. Peanut-butter sandwiches are a terrific choice.

• Stay in the shade as much as possible when you're not hitting. For example, if you hit from the tee, but the group ahead of you is moving so slowly that you would have to wait in the sun to hit your next shot, stand in the nearest shade and then walk to your ball only when the coast is clear.

• Don't use a dry towel to wipe sweat from your hands, as your hands will start to sweat again immediately. Instead, wipe your hands with a cold, wet towel before you hit. Your hands will be cool and dry by the time you're ready to hit.

241 Leave the Left Out

It's raining. You take out your umbrella. What hand do you carry it in?

If you're like a lot of other right-handed golfers, you'll probably carry it in your left. Why this happens is a mystery, but it is a hard fact.

It's also a bad idea, for two reasons. First, this is the hand on which you wear your glove. The umbrella will shelter your left hand, but it will still be exposed to the elements when it might be better off in the dryness of your pocket. Second, the left hand is the firmer hand in the golf swing; it controls so much of the swing. After eighteen holes of holding up an umbrella it's going to get pretty tired (especially if there's wind).

So think twice before you hold your umbrella in the wrong hand.

Branch Management

When you hit into even the thinnest copse of trees, it is not advisable—unless the match situation means you have nothing to lose—to try to hit through any branches.

Over, under, around—yes. Fire away. But on no account should you fall back on that old axiom, Trees are 90 percent air.

They may indeed be, but, as Lee Trevino has retorted: "So is my screen door."

243 Rain Clubs

When you're playing wet fairways, take one club less than you would on dry fairways.

You read that correctly. Even though the ground will be wet and holding, you shouldn't worry too much about having less roll than normal. Most of today's golf courses are so well maintained, in fact, that you don't get much roll in *any* conditions.

When the grass is wet, however, water is likely to get between your ball and the club face at impact. That reduces spin and can give you a flier—as happens when you hit your ball out of rough and grass gets between the club face and ball.

If rain is actually falling, then the rain itself is likely to prevent your ball from flying as far as it would otherwise go. The rain will beat the ball down. So you may have to go back to "normal" club selection!

244 Top of Mind

When you find yourself off the fairway in even the lightest rough, the first thing you should check is the lie of the ball.

There will be other things to consider: your stance, the wind, your yardage, any obstructions between you and your target. But all these mean nothing if you cannot get the club on the ball and make clean, solid contact.

If you have a bad lie—say, your ball is sitting down—then you must think only about getting out safely. Leave the heroics for another day.

If your ball is sitting up, you will have many more options open to you. *Now* you can start checking everything else.

ELEVEN

Strategy Tips

245 Start Slowly

At the beginning of a round don't try to play your best golf. Just avoid playing your worst golf.

Often players do the former. They try to score pars and birdies and end up with bogeys and double bogeys. Meanwhile, they've ruined their swings for the rest of the round.

Bobby Jones once said that for the first three or four holes, he didn't try to score well. He just concentrated on getting the club solidly on the ball and keeping his ball in play. As his round continued, his swing became more solid, his confidence rose, and he was able to play more aggressively and score better.

So remember that fools rush in. Smart golfers start slowly and carefully, and build from there.

246 Stuck Between Clubs?

Let's say you have 155 yards to your ideal landing area. There is no wind, and you have a level lie. You hit your 6-iron 150 yards and you hit your 5-iron 160 yards. What now? Should you hit the 6-iron a tad harder or take a little off the 5-iron?

Two schools of thought apply here:

1. If you're a golfer of even average skill, you should take the 5-iron. Don't hit it any softer. Just choke down the grip a little and swing normally. Your ball will fly slightly shorter.

2. Then we have what we'll call the Fuzzy Zoeller School. Zoeller knows from pro-ams that the biggest mistake amateurs make is in thinking they can hit the ball farther than they actually can, so they're constantly coming up short. So Zoeller once preached that, when you're between clubs, always take the longer one and then *hit it as hard and as far as you can.*

If you're a low-handicapper, attend School One. If you're in double digits, stick with Fuzzy.

In the Bank

When faced with a delicate shot to a green on which the flag is set atop a steep bank, you have only two real options.

One is to putt the ball, but you should do this only if the grass is clipped short between your ball and the putting surface (and be sure to read the grain).

The second option is to use the bank to your advantage. You'll want to take a middle iron, or a club with little enough loft so that the ball will fly low. Choke down on the club, open your stance slightly, and play the ball a little back in your stance.

The idea is to poke the ball firmly into the bank. Hit it just firmly enough to make it bounce up and just over the top of the bank. It should still have some backspin on it and come to a stop quite quickly.

You're correct to think that flopping a wedge shot is another option; but it's not a high-percentage option. The into-the-bank shot is much easier.

248 The Quick Draw (and the Quick Fade)

A few years ago the Wilson Sporting Goods Company conducted research into how a golf ball reacts when hit by a driver. The aim was to find the perfect system for distributing weight around the clubface. With wooden clubs, the weight is traditionally concentrated right in the center (the sweet spot). With modern metal woods, the weight is distributed around the perimeter. What Wilson came up with was "System 45" in which most of the weight is concentrated on a forty-five-degree line running from the heel of the club face to the toe.

What is most interesting, however, is that during its research Wilson discovered that a ball hit high on a clubface tends to fly from right to left, while a ball hit low on the club face tends to fly left to right.

So if you want to encourage a fade, tee your ball a little lower than usual—a quarter to a half inch. For a draw, tee your ball a little higher.

249 To Tee or Not to Tee?

Golfers have a tendency to hit tee shots on short par threes off the deck. Because they hit their short irons from the fairway well enough, players often conclude, Why not hit the same shot?

Two reasons for using a tee:

1. Tees and fairways are different animals. Because of all the traffic it gets, the teeing ground is usually far harder than the fairway.

2. Teeing your ball up even just a little bit means that there is less resistance between ball and club and therefore less risk of a wayward shot. Why would you turn down a perfect lie?

250 Check Your Stance

Have you ever noticed how some golfers take ages to find the perfect place to tee their ball? They hunt around for a spot of pristine turf, carefully insert their tee in it, then lay their ball gently on top of the tee.

Then they stand in a hole.

The most important area to look for on a tee is not where the ball is going to be but where your *feet* are going to be, because it's impossible to swing well if you're off balance.

Bear in mind also that, while your ball must be teed between the tee markers, you do not have to stand between them.

So if the flattest, cleanest turf is outside the tee markers, you *should* stand there—and let fly.

251 The Answer Is Blowing in the Wind

Few golfers know of the best place to look for clues to the strength and direction of the wind.

Most players will throw grass up in the air and watch how it's blown. Fine—now they know what the wind is doing five feet above the ball. Then they'll look at the flag. Fine—now they know what the wind is doing five feet above the hole.

But do they know what the wind will do to the ball when it's in midflight and at its most vulnerable?

The best possible way to determine this is to check any nearby trees to see how the wind is blowing the leaves and branches *at the top*.

This method of reading wind direction is especially useful on short-iron shots, when your ball will fly higher, perhaps even above the tree line.

Hazardous Material

You'll often hear that the best way to take a hazard out of play is to aim right at it, the theory being that the ball will then curve back to safety.

Good advice doesn't come much worse than that.

Let's say a lake runs all the way down the left of a hole. If you start your ball over the lake, it can do one of three things:

1. fly to the right and to safety (maybe)

2. fly straight and get wet

3. fly anywhere to the left and get wet

Notice that on two of the three options your ball will land in the lake.

Now, if you aim well to the right, a ball hit too far right probably will mean a tough second shot. A ball hit straight will be perfect. A ball hooked left may find the lake. On two out of three you're dry.

And if the ball hit to the right *does* find the lake, you'll be able to drop it farther up the fairway than if you'd started the ball to the left over the hazard.

So don't play around with water hazards. Avoid them at all costs.

253 Heads Up!

How can you avoid having your ball move after you've addressed it in strong wind? Simply by not addressing it.

According to the rules, you can be penalized only if your ball moves after you've addressed it. And you are not deemed to have addressed it until you've taken your stance and grounded your club.

Obviously you have to take your stance at some point, *but you do not have to ground your club.*

This is particularly good advice to remember on the putting green, where the grass is shorter and a ball is more likely to be moved by the wind.

254 Dump 'Em

Every so often you should leave half your golf clubs at home. It will force you to improvise with different clubs and make the game more fun.

One day you could carry the 3-, 5-, 7-, and 9-irons, a 4-wood, and a sand wedge. Next day you could carry the 4-, 6-, and 8-irons, a pitching wedge, and a driver. On the first day you would have to invent a shot with a 3- or a 5-iron. Gradually you'll find yourself being more creative with other parts of your game. Golf will then become less of an exercise in statistics and more of an exercise for the imagination.

255 Mix and Match

This can't be done all the time, but it's worth trying if your course gets quiet: Hit the wrong club from the tee.

The idea was suggested by Lee Trevino several years ago. The gist is this: Every so often, on a typical par four of, say, 375 yards, you should hit an 8-iron from the tee. That would leave you a fairway wood to a green you probably haven't approached with that club. In effect, you play a different golf course and learn a new shot.

The same goes with short holes. Try to hit a 3-iron on a 150-yard par three, or 5-iron on a 115-yard par three. Hitting *short* with a long iron is one of the more interesting exercises you'll find.

The idea is to mix and match to learn a new game while keeping things interesting.

Eliminate Those Practice Swings

In one of the most popular hustles on the golf course, a good golfer offers to let a poor golfer hit five balls with each shot and choose the best one each time. By the time the poor fellow is on the back nine, he has played so much golf that he can barely lift the club—and of course, never wins the bet!

The message is the same with practice swings. Apart from wasting time, they also tire you out. If you take more than one practice swing, you run the risk of finishing the round poorly.

A few years ago I played a match in my native Scotland in which one of our opponents took four practice swings. I was sort of shocked at this—the Scots are not known for such shenanigans—and became quite annoyed when after two and a quarter hours we were four down at the turn.

You know the rest. Although the pace didn't pick up, our fortunes did. Our opponent's play grew more and more ragged, and we tied the match on the seventeenth hole. *His* partner saved the day with par on the last.

257 Never Up, Never In

An old adage, but a good one—especially on birdie and par putts.

What it means is that when you have to make a score, you have to give the ball a *chance* of going in, and the only way to do that is to make sure the ball reaches the hole.

It sounds simple, and it is. But golf is a simple game *made difficult*. Getting birdie and par putts—and anything else essential—to the hole is such an important part of the game that at some clubs the members will penalize you monetarily whenever you leave one of these putts short.

And so they should.

Take Two and Stroll

Let's say you have a tough shot out of bushes. The green is 200 yards away. If you take the safest route out, you'll face an approach of 180 yards. But there's another way out—albeit riskier—that, if pursued successfully, will mean an approach of only 100 yards.

Your best bet? Take the long way.

Here's why: No matter the route you take, it's going to take you two shots (at least) to reach the green. So unless you're absolutely incapable of hitting a golf ball 180 yards, you should never risk further danger for the sake of 80 yards.

True, you may make a miraculous escape—the operative word is "miraculous"—and then hit your approach stiff. But it's always a better idea to plan on striking two *hittable* shots as opposed to a difficult shot followed by an easy shot.

259 Think Backwards

The best tee shot begins with a putt.

Here's why: On a par four the ideal tee shot sets up the easiest approach. And the easiest approach is the one that leaves the easiest putt—and that putt is probably one hit from a point below the hole, as uphill putts tend to be the easiest.

So when you step up to hit a tee shot, think two shots ahead. If you want to have a clear shot at leaving your ball below the hole, where's the best place to hit the approach from? When you have decided that, then you also have decided the best place to hit your tee shot. This is known as course management.

There are golfers currently playing the top pro circuits who are brilliant technically but never realize their full potential because they practice poor course management (trying to hit heroic shots, taking too many risks, and the like). And then there are players like Jack Nicklaus. His swing is full of technical flaws and he hits wedge shots not much better than a two- or three-handicapper, but he does combine intense determination with superb course management.

260 Mind Games

Here's a tip gleaned from the crafty mind of Walter Hagen. It might help you win a match or two.

Hagen was a master at match play for many reasons. One was his amazing ability to scramble for par or better from anywhere on the course. Such play quickly reduced his opponents—who more often than not were playing perfectly from tee to green—to mere shadows.

His more famous strategy involved conceding putts. Whenever Hagen's opponent had a short putt—four or five feet or less—for a half, Hagen would concede it. This would continue as the round went on, until the opponent found himself standing over a short putt for a half *late in the round.*

The opponent would look expectantly at Hagen, but The Haig would stand and stare off into the distance. Now the opponent was faced with not only a crucial short putt but also *his first short putt of the day.*

Hagen's opponents rarely made such putts.

261 Live with Mistakes

Walter Hagen used to say that he expected to hit four or five bad shots during a round.

So if five mistakes did not upset one of the greatest players who ever lived, why does the average golfer get bent out of shape because of one or two?

Golf is a difficult game to play well but an easy game to play badly. Those who come to terms with this and forget about their mistakes are those who continually lower their scores. It's true that if a golfer makes the same mistake five times, then he should work on correcting the mistake. But beyond that, mistakes are just part of the game.

262 Think in Threes

You should consider all options before hitting a shot. So even if you know that you hit a 7-iron 150 yards, for example, you should never pull out the 7-iron automatically when you find yourself 150 yards from the hole.

It may indeed be the correct club to hit, but it's always a good idea to think one club more and one club less. Perhaps your stance demands that you swing with less power than usual. Perhaps there is trouble in front of the green that you want to take completely out of play.

Thinking in terms of choosing from three clubs is an excellent habit to get into. You might even learn a few new shots.

263 Use Your Tee, Part One

When trouble beckons on one side of a fairway or another, golfers have a tendency to tee their balls at the side of the tee farthest from the trouble (if the trouble is down the right, they start from the left of the tee).

Let's say there is water on the left. Even if you tee up your ball on the right side of the tee and try to hit down the right side of the fairway, you have a huge margin for error. If you push the ball, you'll miss the fairway to the left. If you pull it, the ball will head directly toward the trouble.

It's a better idea to tee the ball at the side of the tee closer to the trouble and hit away from it. Now if you push the ball, you'll be down the right side of the fairway; and if you pull it, you'll be down the left.

In other words, you're using as much of the fairway as you can.

264 Use Your Tee, Part Two

Teeing areas are seldom flat. To ensure good drainage, they must either slope slightly or have a slight crown. Although this would appear to put a golfer at a disadvantage, as a sloping tee obviously can't provide a flat lie, it can in fact benefit the golfer—if he uses the slope.

Let's say the tee is bevelled slightly. This means that in the part of the tee that is farthest to the left, you can stand with your feet slightly below the ball. If you have a tendency to slice the ball, this sort of hook-promoting stance could help you. Similarly, if you want to draw the ball—around a dogleg, perhaps—then this stance will help you pull off the draw.

The same applies at the other side of the tee, where you'll find a slice stance. Fighting a hook? Give yourself a stance that will cause you to slice. Want to cut the ball from left to right? The same goes.

265 Dance with Who Brung You

Learn to stick with one shot pattern. In other words, if you tend to hit the ball from left to right, with a slight fade or slice (as most golfers do; that's why cart paths tend to be on the right side of holes), don't even think about curving the ball the opposite way just because a hole may turn in that direction. And ditto if you hit from right to left with a slight draw or hook.

In these instances you should rethink your club selection to work out the fewest shots needed to get to the hole, and then hit those shots as well as you can with your natural shot pattern.

The top players stick with one shot pattern too. The only difference between them and us is that they *can* pull off the opposite when the moment arises—as could anyone who spent his life pounding golf balls on a practice range.

266 Be Aggressive

You will do your golf game no harm at all by trying to hit your approach shots *past* the hole.

That's because you probably won't.

As we've noted elsewhere, most golfers mistakenly believe that they can hit longer than they actually can and that they can hit maximum distance consistently.

But nearly all golfers fail to take enough club, and even with the right club, they don't always hit the ball perfectly. So they come up short.

Trying to hit long just compensates for the misperception. If you have 185 yards to the back of the green and think you hit your 4-iron that distance, step up and hit it. You likely hit it "only" 175, which might just leave you close to the hole.

267 Team Play

Here are a few tactics you should use when you play your weekend four-ball (assuming you play match play, two against two, that is):

- If you and your partner are on the same line for a putt, whoever must putt for the higher score should putt first, and make sure he gets the ball to the hole. That will give the other player a good indication of the speed and break of the putt, particularly around the hole.

• Always let the shorter hitter hit first from the tee because the chances are that he's the straighter player too. It's a good idea to get a ball in play, and then allow the longer hitter to let out the shaft. If he hits into trouble—as long hitters often do—then you're still in the hole.

• Putt in turn. It's fashionable to putt out of turn in match play. If one player lies close to the hole in three and his partner lies far away in two, the tendency is to say, "Let me make the par and you can have a run at it." But let's say he misses the par putt. Now the player has to get down in two, so he's on the defensive. It makes more sense for the long putt to be hit by a golfer who can relax because he knows that if he misses his putt, either he or his partner can still make par without too much difficulty. And that's because a surprising number of long putts are holed when the golfer doesn't have to worry.

268 Knock the Top Off

Another way to stop yourself from coming up short: Aim at the top of the flagstick, not at the hole.

As you address the ball and try to visualize the shot, imagine the ball coming down from the sky and banging the top of the flagstick. You probably won't hit it; you'll likely come up a little short, for the reasons we mentioned in a previous lesson. And if you haven't missed right or left, you'll likely be close to the hole.

269 Bogey Golf

Some holes simply require too much of a golfer. The seventeenth hole at the Old Course in St. Andrews, Scotland, for example, requires a long-iron approach to a shallow green with a deep bunker in front and a road behind. If you try to hit the green and miss—which you probably will—you're looking at double bogey or worse.

This type of hole, along with long, tough par threes, is a perfect example of a situation in which you should forget about making a routine par and *lay up*.

But don't forget about par altogether.

The idea is to lay up where you have a fighting chance of a chip and a putt for par.

Let's say you face a 200-yard par three. Your real chances of hitting and holding the green probably will be slight. You may also try to force the shot and will end up in all kinds of trouble.

Now, how about your chances of getting up and down from 30 yards? Probably quite good. So why not hit a 170-yard shot?

If you think this is crazy, remember that the great Bobby Jones played the seventeenth at St. Andrews *exactly* this way: He would hit his approach to a flat area left of the green and then chip and putt for a par—and score better than 95 percent of his opponents.

270 Close Your Ears

When you are in doubt about the club to hit for a particular shot, the worst thing you can do is ask another player what he would hit.

As a matter of fact, such a question is illegal (and so is an answer). But friendly games can easily—and rightly—suspend rules of this sort.

No, the real reason for not asking is that no two golfers hit the same shots.

It's true that if you play with someone regularly, you get a feel for his game and can compare it to yours. But if someone tells you he hit a 5-iron, how do you know without further interrogation whether he hit it flush or thin, whether he intended to hit high or low, whether he cut the ball or drew it? There are just too many things to consider beyond the number of the club.

It makes much more sense to go with your own feelings and hit the shot *you* think should be hit. It may not come off, but at least you'll learn something and might avoid repeating the mistake.

271 Aim for the Bull

The favorite saw of Harvey Penick, whose *Little Red Book* brought him belated fame and fortune, is, Take dead aim. And he's right. But what does he mean by this?

Simply that golf is a game in which the best players try to hit targets as opposed to hitting in general directions.

When you stand on a tee, you should decide exactly where you want the ball to end up, and hit it there. The chances are that you *will* hit a general area, but if you'd aimed for a larger area, your ball could have gone anyplace.

Ditto when hitting toward a green. Decide where you want to hit—front, back, center—and then hit at your target. Don't just hope to find some area of the putting surface.

Most golfers remember to work on their grip, their alignment, their swing—and even to check that their golf shirts are tucked in properly. What they seldom remember is that if they can't hit their ball to the correct places, they'll never get it in the hole.

272 Dump Those Doubles

The quickest way for the slightly-better-than-average golfer to lower his scores is to do everything within his powers to avoid double bogey.

Even in situations where bogey is the most likely score but par is an outside possibility, you should play the percentages and settle for bogey.

Why add a stroke perhaps unnecessarily? Because in the course of eighteen holes a golfer with a handicap of, say, twelve or lower, usually has up to a dozen very valid chances at par—four par threes, four par fives, and a couple of the shorter, easier par fours—and a few real shots at birdie. Figure he'll play these dozen in three over par. If he can avoid the doubles on the other six holes while mixing in another two pars, he'll be round in eighty. That's good for a handicap of six or seven.

273 Make a Plan

When playing a match, should you play against your opponent or against the scorecard?

One argument says that you play the course, because what your partner does is completely outside your control.

Another argument is that you play your opponent because he'll be affected by how you play, and vice versa.

Both concepts make sense. Neither is entirely correct. In the vast majority of cases you should play against the course *and* your opponent.

Most matches have a difference in handicaps, which means you either get strokes from your opponent or give them. Before playing your match, you should get your hands on a scorecard and mark the holes where the strokes fall.

When you get strokes, determine whether you can use the strokes where they've allocated. Say you get a stroke on a hole so tough that you can count on scoring double bogey and still lose the hole. You should then find a hole—probably a short one—where you'll have a reasonable chance of winning the hole *without* using a stroke.

Similarly, if you have to give strokes, you should determine where it's safe to give up a stroke—that's the toughest hole—and where you'll have to bear down even if you don't give up a stroke—that's the easy hole.

In each case you match your opponent's skills level to the demands of particular holes—you're playing your opponent and the course.

274 Some Tipping Tips

If you don't belong to a golf club and are invited as a guest to someone else's club, you will have certain services rendered to you and you will be expected to tip. Here are some ground rules:

• When you drop off your golf bag, tip $1 to the young man or woman who takes it for you.

• If you take caddies, offer to pay for their services, and tip them. Pay whatever your host says you should pay. If you pay less than that, your stinginess will reflect on your host's choice of guest. If you pay more than that, your host himself will appear to be stingy.

• Tip $2 to $5 to the locker-room attendant for cleaning your shoes after your game.

Safe, Not Sorry

If you're playing a match and your partner, who has the honor, hits his ball out of bounds, the first thing you should do is put away the driver, forget about a fairway wood, and pull out a long iron.

Your opponent must now hit three from the tee, so he has just "given" you a two-shot lead on the hole. Were you to hit driver off-line into trouble and then have to chip out sideways, you would cut your advantage in half.

It makes more sense to stay fair at all costs to allow yourself to get as close as possible to the green—maybe even on it, depending on the length of the hole—in two. Your opponent will then have to hit two heroic shots to have any hope—and, as he has just hit out of bounds, the chances of that happening aren't too good.

Get in Trouble Early

Let's say you're playing a par four of average length, say, 400 yards, with bunkers and light rough to the right of the fairway and a pond to the left and in the left-front of the green. Where do you hit your tee shot?

If you answer, To the left of the fairway away from the sand and rough, you're wrong. You may have a clean lie, but you'll have to carry the water on your approach. Hit your approach badly and you're looking at double bogey.

If you answer, Down the right of the fairway but left of the trouble, you're correct. It's true that you'll be flirting with trouble, but if you stay fair, you'll have a much easier approach. And if you go in the sand or grass, you'll at least have a *clear* approach.

The message here is that you have a better chance of hitting a green in two from light rough or sand when the approach isn't otherwise difficult than if you have to hit your approach over trouble from a difficult angle.

You should do otherwise only if the trouble by the fairway is so demanding—such as high rough or a deep bunker—that you don't have a chance of reaching in two from that side.

277 Par-Five Smarts

Anytime you face a hole of more than 500 yards you have a tendency to want to bust it off the tee, then bust your second shot at the green.

The strategy for the second shot

makes no sense at all—your chances of reaching a par five in two are slim, and the idea certainly isn't to see how close you can get—but the strategy for the drive isn't that smart, either.

Accept that you'll take three shots to reach the hole. Now determine the spot from which you want to hit your best approach shot. Now determine the easiest way to get there *in two*. It probably means laying back off the tee, then hitting a middle to long iron for a "working" second shot.

Not only will you avoid hazards—they're usually positioned to trap drives—but also you'll have a better chance of staying in the fairway. If you don't do that, then after attempting to reach in two you might be lucky to get there in four!

278 A Mental Tip

This compendium of golf lessons does not dwell too much on the mental side of golf apart, that is, from the strategic approach to the game. Visualizing shots, thinking sweet thoughts, flashing back to wonderful shots of great rounds past—to offer this kind of advice one must understand an individual's mind.

There is, however, one mental nugget that we shall impart, and it is this:

Think your way, and don't hope your way, around the golf course.

Know your own capabilities and play within them; this extends to club selection, ball striking, and shot making. Anything you try to do that is beyond your capabilities—which is not to say that something can't be learned—will be something you hope you can pull off as opposed to something you know you can do.

Those who hope never score well. Those who think score better with each round.

279 4s and 5s

An easy way to keep score when on the course without using a pencil and scorecard is to count "over and under" 4s or 5s.

We'll start with 5s. If you're an average golfer, you probably shoot around 94 on a par-72 course. That's the equivalent of scoring a 5 on every hole, except for four holes, where you scored a 6. Put another way, a score of 94 is the same as a score of "4 over 5s."

You can use this system to keep track of your score throughout the round. If you begin with a 6, you're "1 over 5s." If you shoot two 5s, and then a 4, you'd be back to "level 5s." At the end of the round, count your over or under 5s and add or subtract them from 90 (or 18 times 5).

The better golfer can count over or under 4s, and add to or subtract from 72 (18 times 4). In fact, when it becomes easier to count against 4s than against 5s, you'll know you're really improving.

280 Take One and Putt

When you stand on the tee of a par three you can safely reach—if it's too long you should lay up and chip and putt for par—you should think only one thought: Hit to the middle of the green.

You may indeed possess the necessary shot to get close to a flag that is, say, tucked behind a bunker to the right, or cut in the far-left corner. If you miss, however, you could be in all sorts of trouble—looking at bogey, double bogey, or worse. But if you hit to the middle of the green, the chances are that you won't face too long a first putt and that should allow you to get down in two.

So you didn't make birdie. No matter. Over the course of a round you can help your score in a hurry if you par every par three.

281 Stand Back

When you find yourself between clubs on a par three, remember that you can alter the yardage of the hole.

Although the tee may be set at, say, 150 yards from the center of the green, that does not mean you *must* hit from exactly 150 yards. The rules demand that you to hit from *inside* the tee boxes, but you also are allowed to hit from anywhere within two clublengths *behind* the tee boxes—so you could stretch the hole to about 152 yards (not a lot on paper, but a big difference in the golfer's mind).

So let's say you are uncomfortable about hitting a 7-iron to a par-three green because you fear you may overshoot your target, yet you are not convinced that an 8-iron will get you there. The solution is to take the 7-iron and hit from as far back as possible.

In general, it's better to hit from farther back than to try and hit the ball harder.

TWELVE

Cures

282 The Hookless Swing

There are several reasons why some golfers hook the ball. For one, they could be contacting the ball with a closed clubface because their grip is too "strong" (the right hand is too far under the grip). But the most likely reason is that they're swinging from outside to in.

A quick cure is to change the swing plane so it is more upright. When the swing plane is too "flat," or laid off, the golfer has no option but to swing from outside to in on the downswing.

An even quicker cure is to concentrate on rotating your hips on the downswing. This will clear out the left side and force you to swing more along the target line.

283 The Dreaded "S" Word

A shank occurs when the face of the golf club is left open at impact and the hosel—the part of the club that joins the shaft to the head—cuts across the ball.

Here are two quick fixes:

1. When you address the ball, evaluate your position using a mental checklist. Everything should be square to the target line: your feet, hips, shoulders, hands, and—most important in this instance—the clubface. Concentrate on returning the clubface to that position when you hit the ball.

2. As you approach impact, think of yourself as slapping the ball with the back of your left hand. This will help you square the clubface if you've opened it during the swing, or it will prevent you from opening the face as you're about to strike the ball.

284 The Sky

If you have a tendency to sky the ball from the tee—that is, to hit a short, straight, high shot—you're likely doing one of two things, or maybe both.

You could be teeing your ball too high. Your club is passing virtually under the ball and catching it only with the top of the club, sending it upward.

It's more likely, however, that you're swinging into the ball at too steep an angle. Ideally, you want to hit from a tee either right at the bottom of your swing arc or just after the bottom, when the clubhead is beginning to rise again. When you come into the ball too steeply, you pop it up in the same way that a baseball hitter pops up in the infield when he swings down but catches the baseball with the top of his bat.

285 Stop the Top

No matter what you call the topped shot—some call it a skull or a blade—it results from a common flaw: The golfer flicks his wrists and raises the leading edge of the club just as he is about to hit the ball.

The key here is to quieten the hands. Concentrate on keeping the forearms, wrists, and hands firm—not stiff, because your whole body may seize up—as you hit down and through the ball. (Try to imagine that your wrists are in a plaster cast.)

286 Fool the Pull

Swinging with the ball too far forward in the stance usually results in a pulled shot. The clubface tends to close, which means it is no longer square at the point of contact. The hips tend to clear, encouraging a sort of baseball swing. Think of a foul ball hit down the third-base line and you'll get the idea.

The cure is simple: Move the ball back in your stance. There is no perfect ball position; some golfers advocate the same position for every shot, while others argue that the shorter the shot, the farther back in the stance the player should position the ball. But you'll eliminate the pull by moving the ball back at least to the inside of your left heel.

287 Beat the Speed Trap

Too many golfers swing too fast, when the whole idea is to swing as slowly as possible. Bobby Jones once opined that it is impossible to swing slowly enough. And, it is said, the South African star of the 1950s, Bobby Locke, worked on slowing his tempo by doing everything slowly from the moment he woke up on the day of a tournament. He would get out of bed slowly, brush his teeth slowly, get dressed slowly, and so on.

You won't have to go to such lengths, but it is in your best interests to slow down. And the best way to achieve that is to pause at the top of your swing: Count "one" on your backswing, "two" as you pause, and "three" on your downswing.

Swinging fast forces you to start the downswing before you've finished your backswing. The pause ensures that you keep the two movements separate, improves your tempo, and slows you down immeasurably.

288 The Smothered Drive

You will smother a drive when you position the ball too far back in your stance. As you start your downswing you realize that the ball is too far back and adjust by lowering the right shoulder. This brings the club inside the target line and forces you to "flick" at the ball. Because the club face hasn't had time to return to the square position, it's still closed and you end up smothering the drive and sending it squibbing off to the left.

The cure is simple: Move the ball farther forward in your stance, and concentrate on keeping the back of your left hand square to the target line at impact.

289 Falling Forward

If you tend to fall forward as you swing, it could be that you're swinging too hard, but it's more likely that your balance is off.

To understand better balance, stand with your feet together as you hit a series of practice shots. With this stance it's far more difficult to attain good balance, so you really have to work on it. You have to improve your swing and your tempo—to the point that when you go back to a normal stance, each element of the swing has improved.

290 Still Snapping?

When your right hand gets too busy in the swing, your left wrist can break too quickly and that can lead to a hook.

To get the proper feel for how the left wrist works during the swing, take a few practice swings, but take your right hand off the grip as you hit the ball.

In order to keep control of the golf club, you must keep your left wrist firm. And that's how it should be during the golf swing.

The Right Quadrant

An interesting way to cure a slice or a hook is to aim at a particular "quadrant" of the ball.

Imagine that the top of the ball is divided into quarters, much like the points on a compass. North is farthest from you, south is nearest, west is the farthest left part of the ball, and east is the farthest right.

Now imagine that the underside of the ball is quartered in the same way.

If you have a slice, you should aim to make contact with the ball on the underside, with the quadrant between east and south. That way you'll force yourself to swing from inside the target line to outside.

Conversely, if you have a hook, think of hitting the quadrant between north and east.

Remember, however, that this cure for the hook and the slice requires you to exaggerate the correct angle of attack (which is coming in from just inside the target line, or just south of east). In the end, that's the spot on the ball you should be aiming for.

THIRTEEN

Practice Lessons

Home Improvement

The pattern on a rug or carpet, or the tiling on a kitchen floor, can be useful tools for checking and working on alignment.

Imagine you're in a kitchen with square tiles. The squares form a grid of ninety-degree angles. Take your stance with your toes on a single line and with a perpendicular line running just inside your left heel. Address an imaginary ball with the clubhead just behind the perpendicular line. That would be your position for hitting a shot with the ball just inside your left heel.

If you've been having trouble with alignment—you may *think* your stance is square, but it's really closed and *that* is why you're hooking so much—then just aligning the feet along the seam a tile or the pattern of a rug will allow the rest of your body to feel what a square stance should be like.

293 Be the Firing Squad

Few golfers take to the practice range with a purpose. Or maybe they don't have time to go through a complete and thorough practice regimen. Here's a quick lesson that addresses both situations:

Take one club—a 4-, 5-, or 6-iron preferably. Pick a few targets within range of the chosen club. Try to hit different targets with the club. This will give you an instant feel for different types of shots.

Better still, hit a moving target. If there's someone out on the range in one of these armored tractors that scoop up practice balls, *try to hit the tractor*. You'll be amazed at how versatile you can become in such a short time.

294 The Rhythm Method

The golf school called Swing's the Thing has one of its tutors perform a sort of trick during a clinic. He places half a dozen balls about six inches apart in a straight line running away from him; then he swings and hits each ball, beginning with the closest, and does so without stopping.

What's amazing about the trick is not that he makes such crisp contact, but that his rhythm is almost perfect. As though he were matching a metronome.

Try it. You'll find that the only way you can move up the line of balls is to settle into a smooth rhythm.

295 The Pros' Practice Regimen

Pros always practice on the driving range before they head for the practice green. They start by hitting wedge shots, first the little "touch" wedges and then the full 125-yarders. Then they move "up" the bag, to the short irons, the middle irons, the fairway woods, and finally the driver. Generally, they'll stick with one club until they're hitting shots consistently well with it (which usually isn't that long).

From there they'll go to the practice putting green. Just less than half the shots a pro hits in a given round are putts, so he wants to begin the round with his putting touch clear in his mind.

Pros seldom practice sand shots or short chips from rough, as these tend to be the strongest areas of their games. About the only time they do practice in sand is when the sand they're about to play is of a different consistency from what they've been playing in recent weeks. Short chips are practiced at courses that demand more than their share of these shots.

As an amateur, *you should practice all these areas, however.* Your short games need all the practice they can get.

296 The Tee-Check

The position of your head during the swing should not be overlooked. If you raise your head as you swing back, you likely will raise your shoulders, too, and that will put your swing out of whack. And if you raise your head as you swing down and through, you'll likely top the ball.

Here's how you can test to make sure your head stays on track. Place a tee (the longest one possible) in your mouth just before you address your ball on the practice range. Take your stance with the pointed end of the tee pointing directly at the ball (or, rather, the target line). Swing back, then stop at the top of your backswing. The tee should *still* be pointing at the target line. Now swing down and through, but stop your swing just before your wrists break. If the tee is still pointing at the target line, your head rotation is excellent. If not, then try moving your head back and forth—no club is necessary for this exercise—while keeping the tee pointing at the target line. This is the head position you want when you make your swing.

297 When Not to Practice

Simply put: when you're not playing well. A popular misconception is that if you're striking the ball badly, then you'll be back to normal after a few hours on the practice range.

The fact is, however, that too much time spent in trying to correct a fault can turn a simple mistake into a habit—a *bad* habit.

So how do you correct your faults? Get someone to look at your swing and make the necessary adjustments. Unless the advice is misguided—get professional help, in other words—you'll soon be hitting the ball well again.

Shadow Dancing

If you have a tendency to sway too much during a swing, the first thing to determine is exactly how much you sway. Then you'll know how much work is in front of you.

Place a cardboard box opposite you

so that the shadow of your head falls on the side of the box. (It's best to do this either early or late in the day, when sun is low and casts longer shadows.)

Swing the club back in your normal backswing. Hold it at the top of the swing. Without moving your head, look at the box—or, rather, look to see where the shadow of your head is in relation to the box.

Now swing forward and through, and hold your position at the end of your follow-through. Again, without moving your head, check where the shadow is in relation to the box.

Keep working at your swing until the shadow stays on the box or at least barely leaves it.

299 Heavy, Man

You can make your own practice club simply by applying tinfoil to the head of an old driver.

Of course, you might need a lot of tinfoil. Just be sure to pack it down hard. Now you'll have a weighted club, which is an excellent tool for getting the golfing muscles into shape.

300 Just Don't Use Your Best Bone China . . .

One of the best ways to strengthen the golf muscles *and* get the feel of what a firm, strong swing is like is to swing against an old car tire.

Technically you don't have to use a tire. The idea is to swing against something that won't budge when you hit it, but is soft enough so that you don't injure yourself in the process.

Position the tire so that the right edge is just where the ball would lie. Now, using an iron, give the tire several good whacks.

One thing you'll notice is that the hands are naturally ahead of the club at impact. This is an important part of the swing, because the longer you can keep the hands ahead of the clubhead—which is to say, ahead of the ball at impact—the more power you'll have.

301 Wrong Way Up

Here's a drill for all those fast swingers out there: Instead of taking your normal practice swing, turn the club around, grip it at the hosel, and swing it upside down.

Without any real weight at the end of

the club, it's almost impossible to swing fast—or at least as fast as you normally swing.

302 Lights, Camera, Action!

It's astounding how many golfers own video cameras but use them only for vacations and birthdays. Why not videotape your golf swing?

You'll probably need a tripod, but they're not expensive—and almost every video camera has a screw-in adapter on its underside.

Position the camera so that it records the full swing, and then go through the bag hitting different shots. You might also position the camera to your right, and shoot your swing looking down the target line (this is especially good for working on alignment).

Now you're ready to make all the appropriate adjustments to your swing.

303 Tempo Time

When your swing beings to get too fast, here's a drill to help slow you down:

Address the ball. Start the backswing by lifting the club straight up in front of you until it is pointing at the sky and your hands are directly in front of your face. Your wrists should be cocked.

Now, from that position, make a full shoulder turn and make your normal downswing.

Do this several times. It makes you pause before you begin your downswing, and that is crucial to good tempo.

304 Stay Down Early

After a winter layoff (assuming you *have* a winter layoff), you'll probably be eager to get playing again and will want to hit miraculous shots from the start.

This is not a good idea. It *is*, however, a good idea to start a round of golf carefully, keeping the ball in play until you're confident enough to be more aggressive; so you should start the year by playing carefully.

And the way to do that is to concentrate on staying down throughout your swing.

In your eagerness to start again, you'll find yourself swinging hard and looking up too quickly. Even when your swing is in good shape, this is a mistake, as it can cause you to blade the ball.

So when your swing is rusty, it's an even bigger mistake. Better to be patient and stay down. Soon you'll start hitting the ball consistently.

305 Backup Practice

You'll read elsewhere that the perfectly struck putt (tap-ins not included) should be hit hard enough to roll about eighteen inches past the hole were it to miss. Here's a drill that will give you a feel for the correct distance:

Lay down a club slightly more than eighteen inches behind the hole. Now start rolling putts from different distances. The idea is to make your ball stop past the hole without actually hitting the golf club.

306 Time to Miss

A good putting drill is to deliberately miss the hole. First, pick a spot a good two feet to the right or left of the hole. Hit half a dozen balls at the spot. Now pick a spot about six inches inside the previous one, and hit half a dozen balls to that spot.

The idea is to keep working toward the hole until you have a really good feel for "seeing" the line of the putt.

(Many instructors advise players to aim for spots opposite the side of the hole where they miss most of their putts. So if you have a tendency to pull putts left, start by aiming at a spot two feet to the right, and so on.)

307 Hit the Three

A good drill for practicing short putts is to try to roll them at different parts of the hole.

The idea is to get you to be more precise. Don't just aim for the hole. Aim for the left of the hole, or the right of the hole. When you can do that easily, start aiming for the dead center.

308 Last-Minute Licks

If you arrive late for your round of golf and have but a minute or two before you tee off, use it wisely.

Don't head for the range. You'll end up rushing your practice swings and will probably find a few faults you didn't even know you had (and probably *won't* get rid of during your round).

Instead, you should chip and putt. About half of the shots you take during a typical round will be greenside shots and putts.

So you should practice what you'll need most.

309 The Double-Club Warm-up

Here's a good drill to help you warm up *and* develop a well-balanced swing:

Take two clubs. Grip one club in your right hand and the other in the left (it's a good idea to take consecutive clubs—a 4- and a 5-iron, instead of, say, a 4- and an 8-iron).

Now swing them back and forth normally. They shouldn't touch each other. If they do, then one of your hands is dominant in the swing, and it shouldn't be. If the club in your right hand bangs into the club in your left hand, the right hand is too dominant: Concentrate on using the left hand more. And vice versa.

Soon you'll be swinging with an equal contribution from each hand.

310 Tiptoe (But Hold the Tulips)

Here's a drill to help you keep your weight on your left side when hitting chips:

Take a bag of balls to a practice green. Set up at the side of the green, planting your left foot firmly on the ground but allowing only the toe of your right foot to touch the ground. Now practice your chipping shots.

You'll find it's impossible to put weight on your right side.

311 One-Club Practice

There is a theory, put forward by Tommy Armour among others, that you should practice only with one club, and that club should be an 8-iron.

It's not a theory that everyone subscribes to—a lot of golfers like to practice with every club, for instance. But for the high-handicapper it's not a bad idea because it builds confidence quickly.

When you practice with an 8-iron, or any other short iron, you tend to forget about how far you hit the ball. But when you go to a practice range with a driver or fairway wood, you tend to become too wrapped up in hitting to the farthest flag, or at least hitting as far as possible. The swing itself becomes almost secondary.

As a short iron has a shorter shaft, it requires less effort to meet the ball squarely; therefore you can quickly build a good swing and good tempo—certainly good enough for you to start hitting the longer clubs.

There is an old saying that you can teach a player more in fifteen minutes with a short iron than you can in a day with a wood. Armour's idea is where it comes from.

312 The Poor Door . . .

You can get a quick fix on the importance of hitting through the ball by trying this exercise in front of a door. A word of warning, however: Don't use a glass door.

Stand at arm's length from the door, facing it. Reach out and gently punch the door. It's likely that you're not getting enough strength into the punch to make the door move.

Now, beginning from the same place, punch the door again—but this time step forward with your left foot as you punch. Do you notice how much more powerful your punch has become?

The lesson is this: A golf shot hit with the hands and arms only will not travel far at all. But a shot hit with the lower body leading the swing will fly powerfully and far.

An Easy Workout

It's a sound idea, especially for older golfers, to stretch before a round of golf.

Probably the simplest stretch is to tuck a long iron under your arms and behind your back and then twist your upper body. To stretch the rib cage, raise your right forearm, grab your right elbow with your left arm, and pull across your body (do the reverse with the left elbow and right hand).

A more precise warm-up routine involves swinging a couple of clubs at a time, but gripping them can be awkward. You might want to invest in a weighted club (but don't get one that is too heavy; you don't want to pull any muscles).

314 Mirror, Mirror

Swinging next to a full-length mirror is a good practice because it allows you to check your position at various parts of your swing. Keep in mind that the reflection will be that of a left-handed swing (or right-handed if you're already a southpaw).

When, for instance, you reach the top of your swing, your club should be pointing at the target. Choose a target—an imaginary one, of course—and swing to the top, stop, and then check if you indeed are pointing in the right direction.

You also can check to see if you're standing too far from the ball—you'll be leaning over—and whether your swing is on the proper plane.

315 Learn from Lessons

Every golfer should take a lesson or two at some point: when starting out, perhaps; when having swing problems; or when taking up the game again after a layoff.

But it's equally important to know how to get the most out of a lesson. Otherwise, you're wasting your money.

Here are some pointers:

- Try to take lessons from a qualified teaching pro.
- Decide what you want to work on before you begin the lesson, and tell the pro what that is.
- Listen to the pro. Don't tell him what you think you're doing wrong. If he's worth his salt, it will take him only a few of your swings to decide for himself.
- Videotape your swing. That way you can go over the lesson in greater detail on your own.
- Ask questions and take notes.
- Practice between lessons. And practice what you've been working on.
- Use your own clubs. If you intend to play golf with them, you should learn to play with them too.

316 To School or Not?

Should you go to a golf school?

A few decades ago the answer might have been an emphatic no. Today, however, there are so many schools that no matter your budget, your skill level, or how seriously you take the game, you'll find one that is right for you.

Beginners should certainly attend a golf school. A few days of intense instruction can establish great habits early. Golfers who reach a plateau in their games—they've worked their way down to scoring 85 regularly, perhaps, but can't get to 84—should also consider this type of instruction. And some schools concentrate on areas of the game that count heavily in scoring, such as the short game.

How to find a good school is another matter. Pick up a copy of one of the major golf magazines—*GOLF Magazine* or *Golf Digest*—and check the ads.

317 Confidence Builders

If you're having problems with your putting, you can blame the greens, your putter, the ball, or some weird realignment of the planets. The chances are, however, that the problem also is in your head—you've lost confidence.

The quickest solution here is not to try to bang in thirty-five-footers to prove to yourself that you're a great putter. That will just make matters worse.

Your priority is to start holing putts, for nothing builds confidence quicker than holing putts *of any length.*

So go to a practice green with a handful of balls, drop them about five feet below a hole—or even three or four feet—and start banging them in. This shouldn't be too difficult because these are not difficult putts.

When you can start holing the putts fairly easily, head on to some tougher reads and rolls. You'll be amazed how much better you'll feel and play.

318 When Starting Out

Many beginning golfers are not too eager to practice on the golf course—or even on a club's practice range—because of the "embarrassment" factor. So here are a few tips for practicing at home:

• Buy or rent golf videotapes. There are plenty out there, and while not all of them are helpful, you can glean enough from the most popular ones (by Jack Nicklaus, Lee Trevino, et al.).

- Videotape your own swing.

- Chip into a plastic bucket. Golf stores will try to hawk you practice nets and what not, but a simple plastic bucket can serve as an ideal target. You can also lay down four clubs in a square to make a target.

- Practice putting anywhere.

- Practice your grip. You can do this while watching television; but so you don't accidentally poke a hole in your favorite late-night talk show, have an old club regripped and then cut off the shaft. This tip is especially useful when you're in the midst of changing your grip, because once you've established that change will indeed be for the better, it's then only a matter of getting used to what initially can be a very uncomfortable hand position.

319 A Wrist Regime

Many of the lessons in this book (and in other instruction books) demand that you have firm wrists—for a shot from the rough, for example, or on chips. Or else they'll tell you to cock the wrists at the top of your swing or keep them cocked as late as possible in the downswing.

The point is that how well you control your wrists has a lot to do with how you play and score.

So spend some time building firmness in your wrists. You could do this by working with weights or even by twisting a rolled-up cloth or towel. Just make sure that you take the time to build strength in your wrists.

320 Against the Wall

Practice near a wall if you find that your swing is too "flat"—that is, you're taking the club back around your spine instead of up and over your shoulders, and you're hitting everything with a hook or at least a drastic draw.

Choose a spot where there is a wall close behind you, and address an imaginary ball. Take some practice swings. The idea here is to swing without hitting the wall. Pretty soon you'll groove the correct action again.

Several top players use this drill, the most notable being Sandy Lyle, winner of the 1985 British Open and the 1988 Masters. Lyle had a notoriously flat swing that he managed to get upright, but every time he slips back into bad habits, he heads for the nearest wall.

321 Step Through

A good way to learn the proper right-to-left weight shift during the downswing is to step right through the swing.

In other words, instead of hitting against a firm left side at impact, you should actually bring the right foot off the ground, turn to your left as though you were about to start walking in that direction, and then step forward with your right foot.

This not only teaches you weight shift but may also help you learn a new golf swing. For if you're a golfer who suffers from back pain, then a similar shift in which the right toe stays on the ground through impact is far more attractive than the traditional swing in which the head is behind the ball and the spine curves in a "C" shape after impact.

322 Legwork

When you begin to tire on the golf course, it's your legs that are first to go. And when they get tired, your swing gets out of whack. Then it becomes a vicious circle. Tired legs, bad swing, bad shots, more shots, more walking, legs even more tired . . .

So here's the drill: Exercise more, by running or by riding a bicycle, stationary or otherwise. PGA Tour pros like Raymond Floyd and John Mahaffey added years to their careers when a fitness van began to follow the PGA Tour around. It's also the reason so many Senior Tour players can maintain such a long schedule throughout the year.

So even though it sounds simple, it makes sense: Strong legs will save you several strokes late in a round.

323 The One-Shot Wonder

Take some time at the start of the year to practice only with a 5- or a 6-iron. But don't practice 5- or 6-iron shots. Practice as many different kinds of shots as you can hit with the club.

Apart from learning the principles of all golf shots—how to hook, how to fade—you will learn new shots. The 5-iron and the 6-iron, you see, are two of the most versatile in the bag. They're lofted enough to hit from sand or rough, or similar lies, and still give you good distance.

That is why you find yourself going to them often during a round, and the more you go to them, the more confident you become when hitting them. You figure you're going to score better if you can learn to hit a lot of shots with your favorite club.

324 Up the Middle

Do you play softball or baseball? If so, you're probably familiar with this tactic: Hitters will aim right over second base, so that the ball, hit between the second baseman and shortstop, will fall in safely for a hit.

You can improve the accuracy of your shots by thinking of the batters' tactic when driving a golf ball. Imagine that your ball is teed up on home plate, and then focus on driving the ball right up the middle.

It's all but impossible to hit a softball or baseball over second without keeping the bat traveling down the target line. And that's exactly what you want to do when driving a golf ball.

325 Keeping Count

Keeping a record of how one scores is not everyone's game. To golfers who are content to chase the ball around a golf course without caring much how they score, charting the accuracy of drives and putts and chips is time-wasting, overfastidious, and unnecessary.

But for those who *do* want their scores to improve, there is no doubt that charting how they play will tell them what should be practiced most.

Your best bet is to chart how many times you hit the fairway from the tee. How often you hit the green from beyond 150 yards, and how often you hit it from within 150 yards. How many wedge shots find the putting surface, and how many two-putts and three-putts you take.

Note that we are not concerned with par here. Let's say you hit two splendid shots and face a short birdie putt. If you miss it, you'll still score par; but if you chart according to par, your "chart" will indicate that you played the hole well.

No you didn't! You should be practicing your putting.

The ideal chart measures how well you play the most prevalent shots: drives, the irons, and putts. We haven't included sand shots because you don't normally run into too many during a round—fewer, in fact, than you would imagine—and when you leave a ball in a bunker, it shouldn't take a chart to tell you to work on your sand shots.

326 The Best Putting Practice Aid You Can Find

The shaft and grip look like a putter, but the head is a metal ball, about the size of a golf ball. It's not a popular practice aid, mainly because it's unattractive and uncomplicated—qualities that make it tough to market.

But many top players who are poor (all things being relative) putters use it because it is effective.

Imagine hitting a golf ball with this metal ball. The only way you can make the golf ball roll straight is to hit the back of it absolutely dead-center, on the exact target line. If you don't, you'll hit it off to one side, much like a banked pool shot.

Practice with this aid often enough and you'll get yourself into the habit of making consistently solid contact. As you gain more confidence, you'll be able to practice with putts of different lengths.

FOURTEEN

Equipment Lessons

This chapter will not tell you how to find the best set of golf clubs, the best pair of golf shoes, and the like. Rather, it contains several pieces of advice that *normally are overlooked by the vast majority of golfers*. These are valuable tips that will give you an edge.

327 Carry Three Wedges

Why three wedges and not three drivers and fairway woods?

Because, apart from putts, most shots are hit within a hundred yards of the green—wedge distance. Also, few short wedge shots are identical, so it makes sense to carry as many different wedges as possible. Some golfers playing the PGA Tour carry four wedges (and some have occasionally carried five) simply because they know that the ability to get up and down requires as much skill with wedges as it does with a putter, and that it's the short game that separates the touring pro from the top club players, and the top club players from the rest of us.

Which wedges should you carry? The standard three-wedge set includes a pitching wedge, a sand wedge, and a third wedge (also known as the finesse wedge), which has even more loft than a sand wedge—from sixty to sixty-four degrees.

We won't go into the pitching and sand wedges here; they're standard clubs and if they don't come with full sets of irons, matching versions are available.

The third wedge, however, is rarer but worth seeking out. It is designed to let you hit high soft shots from tight lies. It also allows you to land the ball softly and stop it when you do not have much green to work with.

328 Rough 'Em Up

Golfers with access to a pro shop can have their grips changed on the spot. Others can rub their grips with sandpaper to keep them "grippable" until they are changed.

Don't use coarse sandpaper, because you're not trying to get rid of the grip. You'll want a finer version—just rough enough to scrape the surface. First wash the grips in hot, soapy water to remove the grime and grease. Let them dry and then rub them with the sandpaper.

Remember, however, that this is a temporary measure. When your grips become smooth again, it's time for a proper regripping.

329 Always on Hand

How many times a year do you play in really wet weather? Twice? Three times? Whatever the total, it is probably fewer times than you think.

In such conditions, keeping a grip on the club is almost impossible—even if you wear one of those so-called wet-weather gloves that are supposed to grip better the wetter they get. So it's a good idea to store your old gloves for use during a really rainy round.

A glove becomes unusable when it is too smooth to keep hold of the grip in good weather. But in really wet weather a "fresh" old glove is better than a wet new one. So if you keep changing gloves, you'll at least have some semblance of a grip.

330 Toss the Long Irons

Most sets of irons sold today begin with either the 2-iron or the 3-iron and go up to pitching wedge. But few golfers can hit a 2-iron or 3-iron consistently well—and the best thing they can do with these clubs is to find a cosy corner of a garage and stash them there.

It makes much more sense to carry a five-wood (metal is preferable and most prevalent). The club is shorter and easier to control; it has more loft and so gets the ball in the air more easily; and its wide head pushes down rough as you swing, whereas irons tend to get snagged. It is also useful for long approaches because it flies about ten yards farther than a 3-iron shot and on a higher, softer trajectory, which means that it can better negotiate the hazards that typically cluster around the green.

The 5-wood sometimes is perceived as an "old man's club," but those who make this claim forget, for instance, that Raymond Floyd used a 5-wood very effectively in winning the Masters in 1976. The truth is that no one with a double-digit handicap should go near a golf course without a 5-wood.

331 Make the Most of Them

The rules permit you to carry up to fourteen clubs. They don't say *which* fourteen to carry, so we'll do that for you.

Carry only those clubs you know how to use, and then complement them with clubs that on occasion you might *have* to use.

The clubs you probably don't know how to use are the long irons. As for clubs you might have to use, you may want to carry a left-handed club, because you never know when you may have to hit southpaw next to a tree, wall, or bush.

Or you may want to carry two putters; a heavy one for long uphill putts and a light one for downhill putts.

There are even those golfers who carry two clubs of the same denomination, two 5-irons perhaps. Although there's no concrete logic for this, the golfers who do so are content with their makeup, and that's important. If they think it helps their game, it probably does if for no other reason than that it boosts confidence.

332 Which Ball for You?

Golf balls have come full circle. More than a century ago everyone played the same type of ball: a leather ball stuffed with feathers. Then everyone switched to a rubber ball. As time went on, balls came to be very different, with the market dominated by "two-piece" balls, in which an outer casing covered a single, solid core, and "three-piece" balls, in which the inside core was filled with some substance (rubber, usually), wound in rubber bands, and encased in a synthetic cover. The two-piece ball feels harder but rolls farther on landing (and is less expensive to manufacture). The three-piece feels softer and spins more, but flies off-line more easily and doesn't roll much at all when it lands (depending on the condition of the golf course).

In recent years, however, manufacturers have been trying to make a two-piece ball that feels and flies like a three-piece ball.

Why is it important to know this? Because the ball you hit could affect your score, and right now the two-piece and the three-piece are still a tad apart. Some advice:

• If you don't hit far, hit a two-piece. The extra roll will give you the distance you're missing.

• If you're playing a hard course, use a two-piece. It will roll even farther on hard ground.

• If you hit the ball far and like to maneuver it, hit a three-piece.

• If you're playing a muddy course, hit the three-piece. You want as much "hang time" as possible.

There is a third type of ball: a three-piece with a balata cover. Balata once was a natural rubber, but now it's a synthetic that nevertheless allows the most feel of any ball. Unfortunately, it cuts too easily.

333 Towel It Up?

Although the size of your grips generally should be determined by the size of your hand, there is a club that should have as large a grip as possible: your sand wedge.

Enlarging the grip, by fitting on an extra-large grip or even just wrapping toweling around the existing grip, will help prevent your hands from closing on sand shots. That's because the smaller the grip, the easier it is for the right hand to roll "over" the left. (You can test this by gripping first a golf club and then something thicker, like a softball bat.)

Sand shots, above just about any others, must be hit with an open clubface, so anything you can do to assure this is going to help your sand game.

334 Your Shaft Should Match Your Speed

Golf shafts come in three basic flexes: flexible (marked "A"), regular (R), and stiff (S). You might also come across ladies (L), extra-stiff (X), and double-extra-stiff (XX).

Your selection of a shaft should be based on how fast you swing the golf club, not on how well you score. The rule of thumb is that the slower you swing, the more flexible the shaft you should use.

Only the top pros can generate swing speeds that merit an S, X, or XX. And if you are a senior or woman golfer, you probably swing slowly enough to merit an L or A. The rest of us probably will do just fine with R.

Remember that swinging the proper shaft helps make the clubhead come into the ball squarely at impact, which is crucial to good ball striking.

Don't Give Yourself the Shaft

We could get into the complexities of shaft length, material stiffness, and flex points, but the message is this: Golfers take care of their grips and their club heads but ignore the shafts that connect the two.

Why? Probably because most golfers believe that only the top professionals can avail themselves of perfectly fitted shafts. Not so. Go to any pro shop or qualified PGA of America professional—the PGA certifies its members—and he will not only determine which shafts you should play, but can also order them and fit them.

The shafts carry the energy from your body to the clubhead and the ball. They also carry the feedback from the shot into your hands and on to your brain. You know when you hit a ball slightly fat, for instance, because the feel is carried up the shaft to your hands.

So getting the best shafts is something that should never be overlooked.

336 Checkup Time

Before the start of each golf season—or at least once a year if you live where you can play year-round—visit your local pro and have him give your clubs a thorough checkup.

He should check the lofts, lies, and swing weights of each club, make any necessary adjustments, and regrip them.

Golf clubs take a beating during the year. They are pulled out of bags and rudely stuffed back in. Some clubs are thrown or speared in the ground after a bad shot. They're tossed down on the ground on a practice range or green. And who hasn't accidentally run over a club or two with a golf car?

It's not as if your clubs finish the year at a forty-five-degree angle, but normal wear and tear merits attention.

337 Heavier Can Be Better

Some golfers attach lead tape to their golf clubs to make them heavier. Here's why:

Increasing the weight usually means more feel in the clubhead, which in turn means more feedback. This is a matter of taste, however, as some golfers prefer, and play better with, lighter clubs.

A popular place to attach lead tape is the bottom of a putter. Again, this could be done to enhance feel, but the added weight is also a benefit when putting on slow greens.

And adding weight to the sole of a wedge helps the club head cut through thick, tangled rough—in the South, perhaps, where Bermuda grass fits that description perfectly.

Keep in mind, however, that irons usually are "frequency matched," which means that they have consistent stiffness and flex points, and adding tape may affect this.

338 A Little More Length for a Lot More Distance

One of the big fads in golf right now is the oversized driver. It has a larger head and a longer shaft to help build up clubhead speed.

But the longer club is not a new idea. For decades smaller golfers have been using longer shafts specifically to widen their swing arc—they tend to have short arms; this helps them build the necessary speed to hit the ball a long way.

So if you need a little more distance, it's something you might want to consider. Although longer shafts are a little more difficult to control, they do tend to work.

Check Your Lie

It is important that the sole of your club lie flush to the turf when you place the club on the ground at address. If it doesn't, here's what may be wrong:

- If the toe is pointing in the air and the front of the sole is off the ground, the lie of your club is too "upright." You can have a pro flatten the lie—bend the toe down—to fit you properly.
- If the heel of your club is off the ground and the toe is digging into the turf, the lie is too "flat" and also can be easily adjusted to fit.

When the sole of a club doesn't rest on the ground properly, the weight of the club won't be distributed properly and it will be nigh impossible to hit the ball solidly on the sweet spot.

340 The Right Amount

The final thing you should do before hitting your first tee shot of a round is count your clubs.

The rules allow you to carry up to fourteen. If you have fewer than fourteen, you're legit. If you have more, then you lose one hole—two strokes in stroke play—for every hole on which you carry too many clubs. (This can lead to the famous situation in which a player carries fifteen clubs for the first two holes, and loses them both, before he discovers his gaffe; he's now four holes down after only two have played!)

You're not likely to be penalized for carrying too many clubs in a friendly match (although don't expect to see the same caddie waiting with a smile on his face the next time you play). Nevertheless, do get into the habit of counting your clubs, because there will come the day when you are playing in formal competition and forget that the extra clubs you'd taken to the range when warming up are still in the bag. . . .

341 Count 'Em After the Round Too

This has nothing to do with the Rules of Golf. It has to do with clubs being misplaced in the normal course of play.

If you use a caddie, and he's double-dipping (as most do), there's every chance that he will accidentally put one of your clubs in the other player's bag, or vice versa. (So count them and *identify* them too).

If you're riding a cart, it's also possible that the right club went in the wrong bag. A more likely scenario is that you will leave a wedge or two beside a green. If you face a shot from the far side of the green from the cartpath, and you can't be sure of your lie, you will probably take a few clubs with you. Similarly, if carts aren't allowed on fairways, you'll park as near to your ball as possible and again take more than one club. Both situations lend themselves to forgetting and losing clubs.

342 The 2-Wood

You don't find many of them around these days, but in days gone by the 2-wood was one of the most popular clubs in the bag. It has more loft than a driver and therefore gets the ball airborne much more easily and it is easier to hit straight. But it has less loft and more shaft length than a 3-wood, so you don't sacrifice too much distance.

One reason for the demise of the 2-wood is the advent of the metal wood whose hollow construction means straighter, airborne hits and just as much distance.

But not everyone likes to hit metal woods. If this is the case, and you seldom feel confident hitting a driver, check your nearest golf shop for a 2-wood.

FIFTEEN

Rules Lessons

343 Cleanup Time

Clean your ball at every available opportunity. Which is not to say, before every shot. The rules don't allow that. But there are occasions when you are permitted to clean your ball, so in the interests of hitting a golf ball that will not have its aerodynamic properties fouled up by mud, it's a good idea to learn the most common ones:

- You are on the putting green (the most important, and frequent, occasion).

- You are in between holes.

- You can't identify a ball as yours. However, you must clean it only as much as you need to identify it, and you may not clean it at all if it's in a hazard. That's because there's no penalty for playing the wrong ball in a hazard.

- You declare a ball unplayable and take the penalty.

• You are entitled to free relief—say, from ground under repair, from an immovable obstruction, or if your ball is embedded.

Note that you may not clean your ball if you are determining whether it is unfit for play, or if you are required to lift and mark it when it is not on the putting green.

344 Drop Twice and Place

Here's how to guarantee yourself a good lie after hitting into a hazard:

In such instances the Rules of Golf usually require that you drop the ball in a certain position, and one option is to drop within two club lengths of where your ball entered the hazard.

If, once you've dropped, your ball rolls more than two club lengths from where it hit the ground, you must redrop. Now, if the same thing happens again, you don't redrop. You *place* your ball on the ground—and placing the ball is to your advantage, because you can pick a spot that makes the ball sit up and allows you a good lie.

So when you have to drop, pick a spot that slopes enough for your ball to roll into an illegal position. When that happens twice, you get your free place.

345 Tee for Two

When you hit into a hazard or out of bounds with your tee shot on a par three, you have three or four options. But generally the only one you should consider is to replay the shot.

This option is always available, but it's especially useful on a par three, because replaying the shot allows you to retee your ball.

You'll be hitting your third shot, but at least you'll be hitting it from what is effectively a perfect lie. Which means you'll have a fighting chance of getting close to the hole and making no worse than bogey—or the best score you can expect after hitting a wayward tee shot first time up.

346 In or Out?

If your ball lies close to an area marked as out of bounds, do you really know whether it's in or out?

Probably not. Yet you can save yourself two strokes if you know not to declare a ball out of bounds when it actually isn't.

If out of bounds is marked by a white line, the inside of the line is the margin. The line itself is out of bounds.

Where it is marked by stakes, the inside of the stakes is the margin. The stakes themselves are out of bounds.

A ball that is on the line—or on the imaginary line between the stakes—is not necessarily out of bounds because the entire ball must rest the line on or beyond for it to be out. So if your ball comes to rest close to out of bounds, check to see if perhaps even the slightest part of the ball is not inside the line.

The Great Stakeout

Stakes on a golf course come in three colors. Two of the colors can be removed if they interfere with your stance or swing, so it pays to know which is which.

- White stakes define out of bounds. They may not be removed.
- Red stakes define lateral water hazards (so named because they usually are set to the sides of a hole). They may be removed.
- Yellow stakes define water hazards (the ideal line to the hole usually has to cross them). They also may be removed.

Note that if you do remove a white stake, but replace it before hitting your shot, you still are subject to a two-stroke penalty. So don't touch 'em.

348 Use Your Length

When you are taking relief—free or otherwise—the area in which you must drop your ball is defined by one or two clublengths. The proper procedure is to take a club and lay it on the ground. For two clublengths, roll it over again.

Here's our lesson: Use as long a club as you can to maximize the area where you're about to drop.

The rules require that you use the club with which you will feasibly hit the ensuing shot, so it would be a bit unsportsmanlike to pull out one of those press-to-the-chest long putters to measure a relief area two hundred yards from a green. In such a case, use your longest club.

For short shots you have greater leeway. If your relief is next to a green, don't reach for the wedge. Go for a long iron, because that *is* a feasible club for a chip.

349 A Little Extra Practice

The rules ban practice during a round, except in certain places. So if you know those places, you'll be able to put in a little bit of extra practice.

You are allowed to practice your putting or chipping on the green of the hole you have just completed—but only if you don't hold up play. You also are allowed to practice chipping and putting on the teeing ground of the next hole.

So the next time that several groups are backed up on a tee, you should practice your short game. Just make sure you stay on the teeing ground.

350 On the Loose

If ever you are required to drop your ball (after taking relief, perhaps), be sure to clear away any loose impediments before you drop.

Loose impediments are defined as natural objects, such as stones, leaves, twigs, and branches, that are not fixed or growing, are not solidly embedded, and do not adhere to the ball. They may be removed; but if your ball moves when you are removing any loose impediments *within one clublength of the ball,* then you are penalized one stroke and must replace your ball.

So when it comes time to drop, it makes no sense to drop and *then* clear away the loose impediments; you're liable to move your ball. It does, however, make perfect sense to clear all the loose impediments out of the way first.

351 A Matter of Length

The Rules of Golf are full of situations in which you must drop your ball either one clublength or two clublengths from a particular spot. Problem is, few golfers can ever remember when to do what.

Here's a simple way to remember: If you are dropping after incurring a penalty (one or two strokes), then you most drop within *two* clublengths of the spot. And if you are getting free relief, then you must drop within one clublength of the spot.

It's that simple.

352 Run Up the Flag

Whenever you face a blind shot to a green, you should ask your caddy to indicate the location of the hole by holding the flag above the horizon.

This would seem to run contrary to the rule that deems it illegal for anyone to stand on the line when a shot is being played. But few golfers realize that there is *one* exception to that rule—and that is when the flag is being held up.

Be aware, however, that if the flagstick is held up to indicate the line of play but *not* the position of the hole, it may not be held up during the stroke.

353 Good Advice

It is illegal to seek advice from an opponent during a game of golf. It also is illegal to dispense advice. (Friendly matches usually ignore this rule.)

But you can get help, because not every piece of information is considered advice.

For instance, while it is illegal to seek help with your swing or to ask a player what club he used before you hit you own shot, it is not illegal to ask him how far you lie from the hole, where the hole is positioned, or where any hazards may be located.

This is considered public information. So if you have any doubts about such matters, feel free to ask someone who might know.

354 No Advice

While it is illegal to ask a player what club he hit before hitting your own shot, it is not illegal to work it out for yourself.

If the player is carrying a full set of clubs, just check to see which one is missing.

Two caveats:

1. You may not commit a physical act in doing your detective work. If there's a towel over the player's clubs, you may not remove it.

2. Knowing what club he hit is not necessarily helpful. You won't know, for instance, *how* he hit it. And that can matter a lot.

355 Know the Ropes

It is a good idea to bone up on the rules. Unfortunately, the rules are so dull, they are a tad forbidding. But two other options are open to you.

The first is to get your hands on a copy of *Golf Rules in Brief.* It's an official brochure that boils the rules down to the most important ones.

The second option is to get yourself a copy of the rules and bone up only on the "Definitions" section at the front of the book. It is here that you can find just what is and what isn't a loose impediment, what constitutes casual water, and more. You may know that you get free relief from ground under repair, for example, but do you know what constitutes ground under repair?

Both publications are available from the United States Golf Association, at (908)234-2300.

356 What Is Casual Water?

Casual water is a temporary accumulation of water on a golf course—rainwater, usually—from which you are entitled to relief. How one recognizes it is another matter.

The popular way to test for casual water is to press down on the ground with the foot. If water comes to the surface, the player gets relief in the nearest dry area. But this is illegal.

The correct way to test for casual water is to take your normal stance as you would play the ball. If water appears, you are entitled to relief (drop your ball within two clublengths of the nearest point of relief, no closer to the hole).

Most weekend groups play fast and loose with the casual-water rule, with little damage done to friendships or golf games. In more formal competition you should observe correct procedure.

357 A Few Lessons in Etiquette

1. Don't talk when another player is hitting.

2. Be ready to play when it is your turn.

3. If you're looking for a ball, wave the players behind you through.

4. If the group behind you has fewer players than your own, wave them through.

5. Rake bunkers after you've played from them—and that includes parts left unraked by *other* players.

6. Leave rakes *in* bunkers.

7. Replace all divots. If you're playing a course that supplies dirt and seed for that purpose, be sure to pour them into the divot holes.

8. Repair ball marks on a green before you putt. Repair *all* marks, including spike marks, before you leave the green.

9. Shout "Fore" if there's the remotest chance that you might hit into another group on the course. And be sure to *shout.*

10. Don't cheat. Play your ball as it lies.

11. If you lose, pay off your bets quickly.

SIXTEEN

Some Lessons for Speeding Up Play

358 Hit the Provisional

When you think your ball may be lost or out of bounds, always hit a provisional ball.

The correct procedure is to tell the other golfers in your group that you intend to do so, then hit it once everyone else has hit. You should then go to look for your original ball. If you cannot find it, continue the hole with the provisional.

If you don't hit your provisional well, you can continue to play it as a provisional until it becomes the "ball in play." This happens when you declare the original ball lost or out of bounds, or when you hit the provisional either from where the original ball was likely to be or from a spot closer to the hole than it was likely to be.

The important thing to remember, however, is that playing a provisional ball *saves time*. If you do not play a provisional, and your original ball is indeed lost or out of bounds, then you will have to traipse back to the original spot from where you hit, and play again—holding up play for everyone.

359 Wait to Mark

If you're keeping score, wait until you reach the next tee before marking your scorecard.

And if you have the honor on the next tee—it's your turn to hit—either hit and then mark the scores for the previous hole or defer the honor. Remember that there is no penalty for playing out of turn unless there is some form of conspiracy going on—and speeding up play does not constitute conspiracy.

360 Park Ahead

If you're riding in a golf car, be careful to park the car at a spot where it won't interfere with the group behind.

For instance, if the next tee is off to the right of the green you're approaching, never drive over to the left. Park on the right, take the necessary clubs, then walk over. The other players in your group can proceed with their own shots as you walk over.

For a group following you, there's nothing worse than having to wait while some slowpoke returns his clubs to his golf bag and then drives across the fairway in front of the green—just to get to where he should have parked in the first place.

361 Let Shortie Go First

When you're sharing a golf car, always let the shorter hitter off the tee play his second shot first. Drive him to his ball—or let him drive you—wait until he selects his club, and then take off in search of your own. While you're preparing and hitting your own shots, he can be catching up to you by foot.

362 Wave 'Em Up

When your ball may be lost and you have to look for it, wave through whoever is playing behind you. There are three reasons for this:

1. The Rules of Golf allow you five minutes to look for a lost ball. Unless you're made of money and in love with losing matches or with high scores, you should use all five.

2. It keeps play moving for everyone else on the golf course.

3. Players who have been waved through always hit their worst shots of the round when the wavers are standing there watching. No one knows why this happens, but it happens to be hilarious.

363 Be Prepared to Play

Preparation cannot be overemphasized. When another player in your group is hitting a shot, you should be getting ready to hit yours.

If you're on the tee, you should be planning where you will tee your ball and where you intend to hit it. You should already have chosen your club.

On the fairway you should be working out yardage and making your club selection. You might even want to take a practice swing. (As farthest from the hole hits first, make sure you are not in the other player's way.)

On the green you should be reading your putt from different angles, stopping only as the golfer who is to putt plays away.

And once you've completed the hole, you should start the process again.

364 Ready, Steady, Go

If you have the honor on a golf course, hit away and then return immediately to your golf car. That way you'll be ready to head forward as soon as your driving partner has hit (or as soon as anyone left in your group has hit). It always makes sense to be prepared well ahead of time.

365 Take the Rake

When you go into a bunker to play a bunker shot, take a rake with you and lay it down on the sand. (Don't stick its handle into the sand, however; that constitutes a testing of the sand and would subject you to a penalty.) When you hit out of the bunker, you'll be ready to rake; rake only those footprints made when you walked to your ball and back. (Had you not taken the rake with you, you would have had to rake an extra set of footprints.)

Should you be unable to extricate your ball from the bunker and it comes to rest against the rake, move the rake, then *drop* the ball as close as possible to where you picked it up.

Index